Critical Guides to French Texts

Critical Guides to French Texts

EDITED BY ROGER LITTLE, †WOLFGANG VAN EMDEN, DAVID WILLIAMS

MAUPASSANT

Quinze contes

Trevor A Le V Harris

Maître de Conférences
Université François-Rabelais, Tours

London
Grant & Cutler Ltd 2005

© Grant & Cutler Ltd 2005

ISBN 0 7293 0447 7

DEPÓSITO LEGAL: V. 2.038 - 2005

Printed in Spain by
Artes Gráficas Soler, S.L., Valencia
for
GRANT & CUTLER LTD
55–57 GREAT MARLBOROUGH STREET, LONDON W1F 7AY

Contents

For Isabelle

Note

All quotations from *Quinze contes* are from the Cambridge University Press editon of the stories, edited by F. C. Green, first published in 1943, but regularly reprinted since. Each reference is given simply as a page number in brackets after the quotation.

1. Introduction

Guy de Maupassant (1850–93) did not come from a rich family. His aristocratic name should not lead us to assume he was heir to a great fortune or an estate. His parents, indeed, often struggled. And were it not for the fact that his mother was a close friend of Gustave Flaubert (1821–80), Maupassant might never have become a writer at all.

He did, however, have one great natural asset: energy. He spent the greater part of his childhood outdoors — walking, swimming, rowing — and consequently developed a strong constitution which was almost certainly a factor in allowing him to publish a great deal in what was a relatively short literary career. Broadly speaking this covered the period from 1880 to 1890. It was a period during which Maupassant produced: two, sometimes three long articles or 'chroniques' per month for fashionable Parisian newspapers; a short story every two weeks (many of the stories being, in fact, rather long); a novel, on average, every eighteen months. And these are only the main aspects of his work. In addition, for much of the period concerned, he had a full-time job as a civil servant... By any standards, this is a busy life.

Perhaps because of his amazing work rate many critics have tended to assume that Maupassant's writing cannot be profound: an author who writes so much so quickly, it is argued, is bound to be superficial. Indeed, the most lasting tag which has been attached to Maupassant's work over the years is that it is 'simple'. Most readers of Maupassant's short stories would probably agree. But the consequences of that simplicity, where critics and students are concerned, have not always been good for Maupassant's literary reputation. Although it is true to say that he has a more enthusiastic following in Britain and America than he has in France (where the short story as a genre does not enjoy such a high status), he has usually been thought of everywhere as someone able to produce narratives easily and to produce easy narratives. This reputation has stuck: apparent ease of composition and undoubted ease of reading combine to make of the typical Maupassant story a form of literature which is not quite serious, not quite complex enough to be considered as 'great' literature.

What constitutes 'great' literature, of course, is very difficult to define. Arguments are not rare and there have always been dissidents where Maupassant is concerned: Gustave Flaubert, for one, was convinced that *Boule de suif* (Maupassant's first major story, published in 1880) was a masterpiece. No less a figure than Henry James (1843–1916) thought most highly of Maupassant's work, not least the novel *Pierre et Jean* (1887). But Maupassant's reputation is such that even when one wants to compliment him, it can occasionally backfire. F. C. Green, for example, discussing the same novel in the introduction to his edition of *Quinze contes,* argues that, 'When he chose, Maupassant could write a first-rate novel'. Despite Green's good intention, 'first-rate' is a notorious platitude for 'good' and amounts to damning Maupassant the novelist with faint praise. Green soon finds himself drawn back to more familiar territory, praising Maupassant for 'his love of form, his instinct for clarity and conciseness, his flair for the truly dramatic situation'. In other words, the author's apparent talent is merely the automatic translation of natural gifts and there is no real merit attached to his composition, since the act of writing, in some sense, is effortless...

While I shall be leaving aside the detailed and difficult debate concerning the precise relationship between simplicity and shallowness, my intention is to attempt to show that it is none the less dangerous to dismiss Maupassant as a minor author on the basis of the apparent simplicity of his writing and, correspondingly, to point up something of the intricacy of his work. In doing so, I am not interested in rehabilitating Maupassant in the eyes of the literary establishment, but merely trying to emphasise to students and other readers of his work that it is worth asking ourselves a few questions about this fluid, straightforward writing, since the answers will, above all, enhance our pleasure, as well as giving us considerable insights into the society Maupassant was writing about.

In the brief study of *Quinze contes* which follows, rather than deal with each story in turn (an approach which would have led me to repeat myself too frequently), I have chosen to group all my remarks about the different stories under each new chapter heading: the comments, therefore, all move in the same direction and explore a given aspect of Maupassant's short story technique. Inevitably I have given more attention to some stories than to others, but I have tried to show that, whatever the apparent interest or merits of each narrative, they all illustrate, to differing degrees, those points which give a fundamental unity to Maupassant's writing.

2. Themes

Maupassant's massive short story output means that it would be difficult to find a theme which he does not address at some time or another. To some extent this is an effect of the law of averages. It is also understandable, since any writer — lowly or lofty — wishes to demonstrate that s/he can be comprehensive. But this is not the only reason for Maupassant's breadth of vision, nor even the most important one. In addition, the kind of coverage which Maupassant achieves, reflects the predominantly documentary nature of prose fiction during the years when he was writing. It would, of course, be a mistake to think that 'realism' (used in the broadest sense to describe works which portray a recognisable, believable world) was the only mode of representation available to Maupassant. Indeed, there were many competing schools and movements: for example, impressionist, post-impressionist and 'pointilliste' painting, and symbolist poetry and music. However, realism, in the sense of 'realistic' writing (and drama), still occupied a dominant position and writers who aspired to any measure of seriousness in this area still assumed many of those duties of documentation we now readily associate with history — which was becoming well-established as a science at that time — or sociology — only just beginning to emerge. Arguably, the writer who epitomised the documentary approach to prose fiction at this time was Emile Zola (1840–1902), the main vehicle being his vast *Rougon-Macquart* cycle, a series of twenty novels published between 1870 and 1893. As we can see, the years covered by *Quinze contes*, that is 1880–86, fall squarely within Zola's active period.

Maupassant, then, was working at a time when writers of realistic fiction were still in pursuit of what one could term a universalist ideal. And Maupassant, like his contemporaries, held sufficiently to this ideal to embrace a wide range of subjects in his stories. And yet, just as the potentially dull details amassed by a figure like Zola are always brightly lit by his powerful and highly personal vision, so the themes Maupassant explores are subjected to his own unifying world view. It is this vision which organises the apparently fragmentary work of the producer of myriad short narratives into a genuine 'œuvre', and which colours the treatment of each different theme. It is the thematics of *Quinze contes* which I propose to look at now.

Town and Country

Much of the detail of Maupassant's world view will, I hope, come more sharply into focus as this brief study develops. One thing is very clear right from the opening story of the collection. Namely, that Maupassant sees Parisian society as a hypocritical, frivolous and often farcical business, though the humour, as in *La Parure*, is often a black, bleak laughter. Mathilde Loisel's inordinate vanity leads, in the end, to a kind of suburban tragedy as she and her husband subject themselves to ten years hard labour to pay for a lost necklace which, as readers of this most famous of Maupassant's short stories all know, turns out to have been a worthless fake. One encounters a similar mix of vanity and frivolity in *Le Protecteur*, in which Jean Marin constantly gives in to a 'démangeaison de parler' (15), a desire to tell people of his lofty status as 'conseiller d'Etat'[1], offering spontaneous assistance to anyone who happens to pass by. Marin's vanity, in itself, reduces the seriousness of his political function, since his showing-off signals a markedly amateur attitude to his responsibilities, a preoccupation with pomp and image rather than substance and the correct conduct of affairs. His position is further equated with frivolous pastimes when Maupassant has Marin write letters of recommendation 'au café Américain, chez

---

[1] The 'Conseil d'Etat' is an apolitical, consultative government committee, also doubling as a tribunal in cases of conflict in the French administration. It is composed of the highest–ranking 'fonctionnaires' or civil servants in France: hence Marin's pride (though it is now more difficult to be appointed to it, since it is a pre–requisite that one should be a graduate of the 'Ecole Nationale d'Administration').

Bignon, chez Tortoni, à la Maison-Dorée, au café Riche, au Helder, au café Anglais, au Napolitain' (15): in short, all the most fashionable watering-holes in 1880s Paris. The overall effect of the story is a satirical reduction of the serious to the trivial.

The juxtaposition of momentous events and levity of response reaches a greater intensity in *Un duel*. Here, two nameless, not to say characterless Englishmen, treat the whole ordeal Monsieur Dubuis goes through as an elaborate form of tourist entertainment. They are presented throughout as spectators rather than participants. More-over, when the train carrying Dubuis and the others stops and the duel is fought, the Englishmen are not at all concerned for Dubuis, but make sure they protect themselves from the strong sun and hurry things along lest the train leave without them. A similar situation in some ways exists in *La Question du latin*. Whereas in *Un duel*, however, a very serious matter turns into something of a farce, in *La Question du latin* something which starts out as 'une farce d'écolier' (120) ends up in deadly earnest, as Piquedent, the dusty old Latin master at the 'Institution Robineau', ends up marrying a young working-girl thanks to the mischievous interference of the student-narrator.

The common denominator in all these examples might be described as a lack of respect, an irreverence in circumstances which would ordinarily require a degree of decorum. Irreverence, certainly, is an important element in Maupassant's writing and among his literary ancestors in this respect would be, of course, Flaubert, but also Voltaire (1694–1778) and Rabelais (1494–1553). But, in more abstract terms, what typifies the examples quoted is the inappropriate or, more precisely, the inauthentic response of the characters involved. The inability to react seriously to serious situations, or the tendency to invest frivolous ones with spurious importance, are both behaviour patterns which are inconsistent with the perceived moral demands of the context. The characters do not appear to register this fact and their behaviour is, as a result, curiously contingent, put on, a kind of play-acting. Since the characters apparently lack the necessary code, or set of fully, logically motivated responses, but since they must also, of necessity, react in *some* way, they unavoidably indulge in a simulacrum, a false response.

This artificiality or theatricality is sometimes analysed in a much more thorough manner. When, for example, Mme Caravan the elder dies in *En famille*, Caravan's wife can only come up with 'une crise convenable de chagrin' (33). She realises that it would appear callous to tuck into a hearty dinner only moments after the death of her mother-in-law, and so she is forced into a strategy of comic hypocrisy. Although she is clearly ravenous, she works hard to project that lack of appetite usually induced by grief: 'Mme Caravan, de temps en temps, piquait un gros morceau au bout de sa fourchette et l'avalait avec une sorte d'inattention étudiée' (35). By contrast, Chenet, the quack who declares Mme Caravan dead, displays an hypocrisy devoid of all scruple. On the point of leaving Caravan's flat, he hesitates and subsequently engineers an invitation to dinner, 'se servant lui-même, [puisant] trois fois dans le plat' (35).

En famille — in many ways the centrepiece of *Quinze contes* — is also important in the sense that Maupassant uses the 'figuration qui doit accompagner la Mort' (34) to point up the artificial, ritual nature of behaviour in general. He does this by having Caravan's two children, Marie-Louise and Philippe-Auguste, perform a simulacrum of a simulacrum as they imitate 'les simagrées maternelles' (46) at the bedside of their 'dead' grandmother. By having the children perform in this way, Maupassant conveys two important concepts. First, the children's imitation of their mother's deathbed ritual is, as far as the children themselves are concerned, a perfectly sincere recreation. That is, they are indulging in spontaneous play, pure ludic activity. Second, while their game emphasises their mother's hypocrisy, it nevertheless underlines the similarities, for Maupassant, between children and adults. Popular psychology might advise us that, in any event, adults are only grown up children, but Maupassant's deft sleight of narrative technique lends a certain resonance to this idea. He reminds us, above all, that human beings are essentially social animals who have need of play, ritual and routine. Men and women who live in urban surroundings, however, live those routines and rituals in an impoverished, reduced mode. Monsieur Caravan, for example, has led an existence of quite stultifying ordinariness:

> Depuis trente ans, il venait invariablement à son bureau, chaque matin, par la même route, rencontrant à la même heure, aux mêmes endroits, les mêmes figures d'hommes allant à leurs affaires ; et il s'en retournait, chaque soir, par le même chemin où il retrouvait les mêmes visages qu'il avait vu vieillir (26).[2]

But it is not only Caravan's routine existence as a commuter which interests Maupassant, although, in itself, his analysis of this comparatively new sociological phenomenon is worthy of some note. Maupassant is also concerned to point up the moral impoverishment engendered by this urban to-ing and fro-ing, an existential shallowness signalled by the ironical use of such terms as 'compagnon' to describe Chenet and 'ami' to describe the owner of Caravan's local bar: the first, after all, abandons Caravan at a critical moment of grief, the second registers Caravan's announcement of his mother's death with 'un "Ah!" distrait' (39): neither response can easily be confused with genuine sympathy or friendship.

Maupassant has a tendency to see such characteristics as predominantly Parisian and it is clear that he was conscious of the fact that France in the 1880s was reaching the high point of its industrial revolution: the 'poussière blanche ... opaque, suffocante et chaude' (25) which so bothers the passengers on the Neuilly tram in the opening lines of *En famille* is an early forerunner of urban traffic pollution. But Maupassant was at least as interested, if not more so, in the French countryside during this period and the characters and situations of the more 'provincial' stories create a

---

[2] Maupassant devotes one of his 'chroniques' to the theme of 'Les Employés' where he talks in similar terms of the drudgery of the average ministry post : 'On pénètre là à vingt ans. On y reste jusqu'à soixante. Et pendant cette longue période, rien ne se passe' (*4*, 1, 377–78).

fundamental contrast. In terms of social and economic history, Maupassant's accounts of provincial life are a valuable document concerning the transformation of France, following a massive rural exodus, into what became known half a century later as *Paris et le désert français*.[3] For a sociologist or a social historian, *Quinze contes* provides useful confirmation of important facts about certain types of infrastructure. We can deduce, for example, basic data about the transport and communications system in France at that time: in *Un coup d'Etat*, the newspapers carrying the news of the military defeat at Sedan, have taken a full day to reach the Normandy village in which Massarel and Varnetot play out their farcical power struggle.

Maupassant, however, although he is clearly fascinated by the movement of history, is also struck by the profound contrasts between, on the one hand, the hectic life of Paris and the new suburbia under its 'buée rouge' giving out 'une sorte de roulement continu' (37) and, on the other, the unchanging life of the countryside and villages. Maupassant sees this profound rural permanence in such things as attitudes to death, 'cette indifférence du paysan pour la mort, fût-il son père ou sa mère, cet irrespect, cette férocité inconsciente si communs dans les campagnes, et si rares à Paris' (36). Country people have the same uncomplicated approach to the living human body. In *Le Baptême*, for example, after the christening ceremony, Maupassant's description of the endless eating is punctuated with references to 'la lourde gaieté campagnarde [qui] éclata comme une tempête', or 'des gros mots, fortement salés' (72), or 'des propos polissons' (73): the whole christening feast seems to be one long succession of bawdy innuendo, with the two sexes almost appearing to contest supremacy in the art. Among the younger generation, although the lavatorial humour may cause the girls to blush, it certainly does not stop them giggling. As for the older generations: 'Le père et le grand-père ne tarissaient point [...] La mère souriait; les vieilles prenaient leur part de joie et lançaient aussi des gaillardises' (73). As if to

---

[3] This was the title of a very influential book by J. F. Gravier, published in 1947.

emphasise the equality of the sexes in their natural habitat, Maupassant sums up the toilet arrangements thus: 'Hommes et femmes sortaient de temps en temps dans la cour, puis rentraient se mettre à table' (74).

Indeed, 'les gens des champs' (72) are assimilated to nature, formed and deformed by it. One old man in *Le Baptême*, for example, is described as 'noueux comme un tronc de chêne avec des poignets bossués et des jambes torses' (70), while the old women are 'fanées ainsi que de vieilles pommes, avec une fatigue évidente dans leurs reins forcés, tournés depuis longtemps par les patientes et rudes besognes' (71). As well as reminding us that pre-Industrial Revolution women shared hard physical labour with men, Maupassant points up the rigid qualities of the peasants' bodies. These, however, are not a sign of atrophy or lifelessness. Rather, they are the visible sign of a symbiosis between the land and the people, an organic relationship which takes the seasons of nature and breathes them into human bodies. Accordingly, the young and very young are presented as 'rose et bouffie' or having 'la face rouge, les yeux luisants', as though they were inhabited by a bursting fertility.

Fertility, indeed, is often seen as a dividing line between the rural and the urban, since many of Maupassant's town-dwelling parents are childless: Monsieur and Madame Oreille in *Le Parapluie* or, in more elevated, more exotic conditions, the count and countess Baranow in *En voyage*. Even when children do come into hard-up, petty bourgeois households, we are led to believe that they represent little more than a financial burden. In *Mon oncle Jules*, Monsieur and Madame Davranche, having been 'blessed' with two daughters, are reduced to promenading them around Le Havre in a regular Sunday ritual, hoping to attract the interest of eligible young bachelors. The strategy has a limited success, since they find a suitor for the younger girl, while the remaining daughter 'semblait perdue depuis le départ de l'autre, comme un poulet resté seul de sa couvée' (77). Money constitutes a narrative mainspring for many of the other stories in *Quinze contes*, too. Indeed, money tends to be a major preoccupation for the majority of Maupassant's characters here, many of them trodden into a money-grubbing, penny-pinching existence by all the institutionalised meanness and drabness of modern urban life.

But it would be wrong to assume that, by contrast, Maupassant's countryside, given its vibrant simplicity, is akin to some rural idyll. Far from it. Maupassant is quick, also, to spot the straightforward nastiness of peasant folk. There is no wistful allusion to innocent, noble savages *à la* Jean-Jacques Rousseau. *Une vendetta*, especially, is a striking, not to say harrowing example of the calculated cruelty Maupassant feels human beings are capable of committing. The account of the way in which 'la veuve de Paolo Saverini' plots and carries out the murder of Nicolas Ravolati acquires much of its power through the matter-of-factness of the narration. It is because the old widow's actions are presented as quite natural and consistent that they are so frightening, her understated savagery being played out in all its horror by the dog, Sémillante, whose name, signifying 'energetic', is something of an ironical understatement. The chilling simplicity of the last line of the story, the foul deed done, drives home the principle of natural violence: 'Elle dormit bien, cette nuit-là' (13).

Maupassant, although fascinated by such violence and cruelty, and clear as to their destructive nature, also invests them on occasions with a different kind of impact: that of humour. *Un duel* is a good example of how Maupassant achieves his effect with the slenderest of means. He distances us from the potentially serious, dramatic emotions which might be expected to derive from a confrontation of this type. Both the German officer and the two Englishmen who witness events, speak and act in a caricatural manner. Maupassant, in fact, explicitly refers to these three characters as resembling 'trois grotesques d'un journal pour rire' (24). We are further kept at arm's length from any emotional involvement with these characters by the representation of their modes of speech, Maupassant giving them ridiculously exaggerated foreign accents. Moreover, they correspond to national stereotypes which had already acquired considerable currency by this time: the German officer strikes a Bismarckian pose of the 'Deutschland über

Alles' variety, while the Englishmen take 'le fair-play' to comic strip absurdity by giving Dubuis three cheers as they leap back into the train.

Politics

Maupassant's aim in *Un duel*, of course, is a satirical one and has more than a little to do with the fact that the story deals with the Franco-Prussian War of 1870–71, though patriotism is most emphatically not the main reason why Maupassant wrote the story: it stemmed, on the contrary, from a profound cynicism and contempt for war and any kind of institutionalised violence.[4] The ironically titled *Un coup d'État* is another example in the same vein. Applying such a grand epithet to the laughable non-events of the story is a clear, initial indication concerning the author's stance. This is confirmed in the opening paragraph, where the events of 1870–71 are collectively referred to as a form of 'démence' and the actions of France's home guard as a preposterous piece of farcical theatre: 'On jouait au soldat d'un bout à l'autre du pays' (96). As in *Un duel*, the violence — inasmuch as there is any — is portrayed as a clumsy and ludicrous inconsistency as practised by the Dad's Army of 'bonnetiers' and 'petits bourgeois' (96) hastily formed in an attempt to repel the rapid advance of the efficient Prussian army. The principal target of Maupassant's irony is Massarel, the local doctor and soon-to-be republican mayor of Canneville. Massarel's ultimate victory over his royalist rival, 'le vicomte de Varnetot', has a decidedly hollow ring to it, since Massarel is snubbed at every turn by his 'troops' and other inhabitants of Canneville. As if insubordination and ridicule were not enough, Massarel finally reduces himself to a pathetic figure as all his efforts at dramatic gestures misfire as we move from farce to the theatre of the absurd. Massarel fires off shots at a bust of Napoléon III, hoping to shatter it in a great show of republican grandeur. Instead, the bullets bounce

---

[4] Maupassant's thoughts on war (*4*, 2, 292–99) are clear enough: 'Les hommes de guerre sont les fléaux du monde' (294).

off, barely denting the statue and Massarel returns to his surgery only to find an old peasant in search of relief for his varicose veins.

There is little doubt, then, that Maupassant is anti–republican, though it is more doubtful whether political satire is the only aim in *Un coup d'État* and still more difficult to gauge what, if any, Maupassant's constructive political ideas might be. There is at the heart of his political philosophy, if one can call it that, a deep cynicism. Politics are invariably presented as a career for creeps and crawlers — witness the aptly named Ramponneau of *La Parure* — or as a frivolous pose, for example in *Le Protecteur*, where the students in the Latin Quarter 'crach[ent] de la politique en buvant des bocks' (14). Maupassant's cynicism applies equally well to older practitioners, too. Jean Marin's friend becomes a deputy in the Assemblée Nationale 'par aventure parlementaire' (ibid.), that is to say by something of a fluke rather than any native talent. The regime, it is therefore implied, is staffed by amateurs and dilettantes. The Republic, of course, attempts to legitimise itself, not least through a system of national honours. But Maupassant mocks these and displays a clear disregard for such a hollow sham. In the case of Caravan, in *En famille*, for example, his 'longue et misérable servitude' as a minor-ranking civil servant is disguised by the official euphemism as 'loyaux services'. Having clocked up his statutory thirty years, Caravan, as is the custom, receives the 'légion d'honneur'[5]: 'Cette dignité inattendue, lui donnant de sa capacité une idée haute et nouvelle, avait en tout changé ses mœurs' (27).

We can safely assume that Maupassant reserves little respect for those who are taken in by this strategy. Not that political ideas opposing the Republic seem to meet with his approval either. Caravan's brother-in-law, Braux, whose 'doctrines révolutionnaires et communistes' (49) constitute a threadbare programme indeed, is presented in such an unflattering way as to pre-empt any serious consideration for such a primitive specimen: 'un cordonnier socialiste, petit homme poilu jusqu'au nez, tout pareil à un singe' (47). A little further on, Maupassant continues the simian analogy,

---

[5] This is an order of merit, instituted in 1802 by Napoleon, awarded by the French President for civil or military service.

Braux's face being likened to a 'figure de gorille méchant' (48), an image which was very much a contemporary leitmotiv used to convey the threatening physical presence of 'le peuple'. Indeed, we are dealing here with late nineteenth-century establishment anxieties about the possibility of urban, proletarian revolution (which was to become a reality in October 1917 in Russia). Long gone are the days of Rousseau's 'noble savage': an idea dismissed by Maupassant as sentimental nonsense worthy only of a doddery old softie like Piquedent in *La Question du latin*: 'il parlait des fatigues ouvrières avec des phrases de Jean-Jacques Rousseau et des larmoiements dans la gorge' (118). Perhaps the most one dare advance about Maupassant's politics is that he was markedly right of centre, although whether he could be categorised as a monarchist is open to serious question. In the final analysis, Maupassant might have supported a benevolent dictator, but there is at least as much in his work which suggests he was apt to drift towards right-wing anarchism, albeit of an armchair variety.

Science

Quite apart from helping us to consider Maupassant's own politics, his attitudes are not without interest for a broader understanding of his literary ideals as well. His anti-democratic, anti-parliamentarian stance sets him squarely against Emile Zola, with whom, none the less, Maupassant is often compared. The older author's firm belief in the Republican ideal is as alien to Maupassant as Zola's conviction that science was the social force which would help realise the great Enlightenment dream: the perfectibility of the human race. Progressive republicanism and the power of experimental science, the twin turbines of perfectibility as far as Emile Zola was concerned, were nothing more, for Maupassant, than double trouble, proof of the eternal capacity for getting it wrong which dogs the human race.

Chief among Maupassant's scientific pet hates was medicine, a fact amply illustrated in *Quinze contes*. Maupassant, who was to die of syphilis, which he contracted around 1877, had a long and painful experience of treatment for the truly awful range of illnesses he suffered from throughout his life. In 1876, he suffered from chest pains and a bout of facial herpes. In 1878 he had a succession of migraines; in 1880 problems with his right eye and hair loss and, in early 1887, a return of the alopecia. The deterioration in his general health only accelerated with the years. The illness finally began to take a firm hold in 1890 with renewed migraine attacks interspersed with deceptive periods of hyperactivity.

From this point on, it became increasingly difficult for Maupassant to do any work at all and more and more obvious that the illness was terminal. He cancelled engagements as new symptoms, at intervals, declared themselves. By April 1890, he had to dictate what little work he felt able to produce and the author's active life effectively came to an end in the latter part of the same year. The whole of 1892 — after a suicide attempt on New Year's Night — and into 1893, were spent in the sanatorium at Passy, on the outskirts of Paris. He died on 6 July. It is scarcely surprising that someone who had such regular contact with so many doctors and underwent some very uncomfortable forms of medical treatment — he was often bled by his doctors, for instance, by having leeches placed behind his ears — should have developed a circumspect and sometimes hostile attitude towards the medical profession: not least because doctors were so manifestly unable to do very much to ease his condition. But it would be a mistake to assume that Maupassant's critical presentation of doctors and medicine was original or unusual in French literature. If anything, criticism of the medical profession was almost a prerequisite for any French writer worth their salt. In Maupassant's case, this tendency is driven by an all-pervasive cynicism which we have already seen at work in other areas. Chenet, in *En famille*, comes in for some of the most stinging ironies. His 'diagnosis' of Mme Caravan's condition turns out to be farcically wrong and he later backtracks with the most monumental bad faith: 'Je m'en doutais, voyez-vous: et je me disais à moi-même tout à l'heure, en montant l'escalier: je parie qu'elle sera debout, l'ancienne' (49). At no time during his examination of Mme Caravan had Chenet even thought of taking her pulse...

But Chenet should console himself since he is far from alone in his incompetence and ineffectiveness. Madame Simon in *A cheval*, having taken a genuine tumble thanks to the clumsy attentions of Hector de Gribelin and his bolting horse, is perhaps less genuine in her subsequent exploitation of the financial possibilities presented by the accident. Whatever her true motivations, she easily outwits the 'quatre grands médecins' (69) whom Gribelin invites to examine her. Or again, in *En voyage*, the well-to-do doctor who acts as narrator, is just as unable to cure the Countess Baranow as her Russian doctor had been. Massarel, for his part, in *Un coup d'État*, has a down-to-earth, if baseless explanation for the old peasant's varicose veins: 'si vous vous étiez lavé les pieds, ça ne serait pas arrivé' (98)... The overall impression of Maupassant's view of doctors that one gleans, just as with France's political elite, is that medicine is an amateur pursuit and a potentially dangerous one at that: for the patient, at least. And the same would seem to be true of applied science in general. Antoine Saverini's vengeful mother does a passably good impersonation of the experiments conducted by Ivan Pavlov (1849–1936), as she trains the dog Sémillante to produce a savage, conditioned reflex when the appropriate secondary stimulus is applied: namely, 'dévore!' (13).

Maupassant is, then, conscious of the power of science, but suspicious of it. The central role of science in the development of social policy at that time clearly seemed to him to be misguided. And it is precisely those stories in *Quinze contes* in which science is, *a priori*, at a loss and in which the irrational takes centre stage, which are among the most powerful narratives in the collection. Two stories — *Sur l'eau* and *La Peur* — take irrational fear as their main theme. In both, worldly wise narrators who, by all accounts, do not frighten easily, explain in considerable detail how a situation develops to a point where the rational mind, despite its best efforts, cannot maintain its control. Indeed, in many ways, it is the rational mind which thus paves the way for the irruption of the irrational, since the rational mind's efficiency at eliminating natural, understandable causes for the particular events being described, leaves the narrators concerned sufficiently perplexed to admit of a possible supernatural explanation. As a consequence, the narrators are drawn to conclude that the mind is divided in two: 'deux êtres ... sont en nous, l'un voulant, l'autre résistant, et chacun l'emportant tour à tour' (54). In the case of *La Peur*, Maupassant cleverly ratchets up the impact of the irrational aspects of the main incident in the story, by first having his narrator recount a bizarre incident which is then explained away in perfectly rational terms. Elsewhere in the collection, the main character of *Un lâche*, Gontran-Joseph de Signoles, is driven to the ultimate human act of abdication — suicide: and this because he was afraid. More to the point, he was afraid of being afraid and his inability to account for this sudden rush of fear into a life of otherwise unsullied bravery and notoriety, is simply too extraordinary to bear. Like the narrator of *Sur l'eau*, Signoles is brought to a 'prise de conscience' occasioned by the intuition that there is within him 'une force plus puissante que sa volonté, dominatrice, irrésistible' (110).

In this short, opening chapter I have tried to draw attention to a number of recurrent themes in the stories of *Quinze contes*, themes which clearly dominate many of Maupassant's thoughts. What I propose to do in the remaining chapters is to take these initial comments, to discuss and develop them into a more systematic appreciation of the intellectual position, or moral stance, taken up by Maupassant in these stories, a stance taken up in response to what he evidently considered as worrying developments in his society.

3. Character

We have already had occasion to compare Maupassant with Emile Zola, noting that, in their treatment of certain major themes, and despite a tendency to place the two authors in the same school of writing, they are often in opposition to each other. This is also true in respect of their methods of characterisation. The author of *Thérèse Raquin* (1867) and *L'Assommoir* (1877), is famous, not to say notorious, for his approach. In the manner of a social scientist — a status to which Zola more or less explicitly aspired — he bases himself on solid, preliminary fieldwork, on the painstaking collection of empirical data and on the conviction that thorough examination of this material will help us to understand the organisation and workings of human society. Zola's methodology, therefore, combines accurate observation with precise documentation. Although, as we very well know, during the writing process itself, this scholarly preparation is transmuted into something quite different, it remains true to say that Zola, in practice, is committed to an examination of contemporary society and is convinced that such a study is a legitimate contribution to social policy.

Maupassant's way of seeing is very much at odds with Zola's essentially *synchronic* approach: that is, an approach which is interested in how things are at any given point in time. True, Maupassant is just as concerned as Zola to derive universal truths from particular instances. But, whereas Zola claims to uncover laws and make of his fiction an instrument of social engineering, allied to a firmly held political stance, Maupassant writes from a much more resolutely classical, timeless perspective. His concerns — aesthetic and political — relate to the eternal, not the ephemeral. He perceives the existence of social groups, but not of social classes. He seeks less to shock his readers than to please them and to please himself. Taken all round, in spite of being dubbed part of 'la queue de Zola', a mere hanger-on, Maupassant is as far from Zola's 'naturalist republic' as one can imagine. Indeed, on more than one occasion he voiced his scepticism and incredulity about Zola's aesthetic position.

Since Maupassant's concern is with immutable human foibles rather than with the investigation of period-specific social injustices, it follows that narrative material does not need to be sought out according to elaborate tendencies, or by the application of complicated techniques: Maupassant takes whatever may fall to hand in order to pursue his aim. Throughout his brief writing career, Maupassant was to apply the same principle: this explains the increasing frequency in his work, during the final years of his life, of characters drawn from the upper reaches of society, as the author himself floated gradually up the social scale into 'le beau monde', on huge waves of commercial success, popularity and, though less frequently, literary esteem.

The aristocracy, accordingly, does not appear in Maupassant's work until the very last years. Even then there is always a sense, more or less marked, in which Maupassant's contact with the fashionable literary 'salons' of his day never became entirely relaxed or comfortable. The author was often ill at ease in such company, where he could not fail to register the snobbery reserved for him and where he was sometimes the butt of high society jokes. There are, in *Quinze contes*, a small number of representatives of the 'petite noblesse', of those 'noblaillons' as they are sometimes referred to, who have fallen on harder times: those provincial notables who, in a way, were closest to Maupassant himself. But, for our purposes, the period covered by the stories in this collection (1880–86), concentrates on that most slippery of sociological fish, the 'classes moyennes', covering quite a large bracket of incomes through which, during these years, Maupassant was steadily advancing. Although the author himself might have been thrown into something of a temper by the assertion, the fact remains that Maupassant wrote of and from the point of view of 'le bourgeois'.

The term, though used readily, is difficult to define and requires a short explanation here if Maupassant's bourgeois characters are to mean very much to us.

The 'classes moyennes' were certainly not a new social group which sprang up spontaneously in nineteenth-century France, any more than the 'middle-classes' are an exclusively nineteenth-century phenomenon in Britain. Just as it is possible to trace the 'middling sort' of person back over several centuries in a British context, so, in France, 'le bourgeois' has a long lineage reaching back to the seventeenth century at least, Molière's preposterous Monsieur Jourdain in *Le Bourgeois gentilhomme* (1670), being the most obvious point of reference concerning riches acquired through commerce, as opposed to inherited wealth. By the end of the nineteenth century, their social and economic domination was clear. And yet, there remained a number of links with the older, pre-Revolution France: notably between the 'grande bourgeoisie' and the 'noblesse de robe'. Most of the other sub-groups, however, owed their greater or lesser wealth to the increased social mobility confirmed by the events of 1789–93. The terms 'petite bourgeoisie' and 'embourgeoisement' came into general use in France during the 1830s, along with those eminently middle-class values of work, thrift and self-help. François Guizot (1787–1874), perhaps encapsulated the spirit of social mobility in his great rallying cry to the French middle-classes: 'Enrichissez-vous!'

It is almost a truism to say that every move made by the bourgeoisie was governed by economic considerations. Accordingly, the politics of the 'classes moyennes' were opportunistic to say the least. At the time of France's liberal revolution of 1830, many would have been of a 'soft' royalist persuasion, taken to mean support for the junior, Orléans, branch of France's royal line (as opposed to the older, Bourbon, branch whose supporters styled themselves 'légitimistes'). But, as France moved closer to the revolution of 1848 — driven there in no small measure by Guizot's policies — there was more and more of a tendency in some parts of the 'classes moyennes' to hitch themselves to radical elements of the left, seeing in this strategy a quicker route to increased political rights. It was only in the aftermath of June 1848 that the working classes and the bourgeoisie, the worlds of the factory and the boutique, underwent a more or less definitive social separation. If the 'coup d'Etat' of 2 December 1851 was something of a setback for the 'petite' bourgeoisie in respect of its political consequences, then it would none the less be true to say that the general evolution of French society was still working to the advantage of the middle-classes. Liberal progress was moving French society forward. By the time the Third Republic was established in 1870, the middle-classes were living and working in a society whose technological and urban character was recognisably 'modern'.

The 'république des professeurs/postiers/cheminots', a republic made up of 'couches nouvelles' or new social groups, championed by Léon Gambetta (1838–82) was the society in which Maupassant lived, worked and wrote. In political terms, the dominant philosophy of the Third Republic was still a liberal, individualistic one, with the 'couches nouvelles' keen to consolidate their position in the social hierarchy and improve it if at all possible. In terms of the general characteristics of the life led by the members of these middle and lower echelons of the bourgeoisie, order and routine were frequent keynotes. It is only a small step to postulate the existence of a certain mediocrity and, if one is an intellectual observer, to castigate the bourgeoisie for its (real or supposed) lack of imagination or its complacent self-satisfaction. Maupassant's great friend and literary mentor, Gustave Flaubert, viewed all that was bourgeois through an all-consuming, withering contempt. Maupassant himself, with one foot in the 'petite noblesse' and the other — as a child at least — in the life of the Norman peasantry, was bound to be anti-bourgeois, from whichever of the two standpoints he viewed that class. And yet, much of Maupassant's own adult life was quintessentially middle-class. Though also heavily influenced by Flaubert, there is enough rough compassion in Maupassant's treatment of some of his bourgeois characters to suggest that for some of the time the author saw himself as a fellow traveller.

Most of Maupassant's bourgeois *men* — for, as we shall see, he characterises men and women in two fundamentally different ways — are pompous and over-principled: the captain of the Davranche to Jersey ferry struts up and down the bridge 'd'un air important, comme s'il eût commandé le courrier des Indes' (79). They are also often cowardly: not only do their boasts have a singularly hollow ring to them (as in *En voyage*: 'Chaque homme savait une anecdote à son honneur, chacun avait intimidé, terrassé et garrotté quelque malfaiteur' [82]), but masculine courage is mercilessly demystified (as in *Un lâche*). Indeed, Maupassant's male characters seldom manage to stand up to authority. Monsieur Loisel, in *La Parure*, on returning home from the ill-fated evening at the ministry reception, is immediately preoccupied by the thought of having to be on time at the office the next morning. Caravan, in *En famille*, arrives at work every morning, 'le cœur plein d'inquiétude, dans l'attente éternelle d'une réprimande pour quelque négligence qu'il aurait pu commettre' (26). He lives in permanent awe of 'les chefs, qu'il redoutait effroyablement' (27). Caravan's fear of his ministry masters gives rise, later in the story, to a petty desire for revenge born of his resentment and envy: he decides, on his wife's advice, not to notify his superior, relishing in advance the thought of being able to spring a copper-bottomed excuse on his superiors for his absence: namely, his mother-in-law's death. As we know, his plan backfires in spectacular fashion, prompting the bathos of the story's ending: 'Qu'est-ce que je vais dire à mon chef?' (50).

Maupassant's petty bourgeois menfolk are anything but red-blooded stallions. On the contrary, they are invariably henpecked. Caravan's wife, for example, having learnt of the promotion of one of Caravan's colleagues, points out with calm cruelty, 'Encore un qui t'a passé sur le dos, alors' (32). In *Mon oncle Jules*, we are informed that the narrator's mother 'trouvait souvent des paroles aigres pour son mari, des reproches voilés et perfides' (74). Madame Oreille, in *Le Parapluie*, imposes a number of embarrassing 'privations' on her husband who, moreover, had remained all his life in his ministry job 'uniquement pour obéir à sa femme' (88).

This moral feebleness of Maupassant's male characters is often matched by physical flabbiness: one thinks again of Caravan, and his 'figure rougeaude [...] son cou graisseux, son bedon tombant entre deux jambes flasques et grasses, toute sa rondeur apoplectique de vieil employé ramolli' (28–29), or of Dubuis in *Un duel*, and the 'poids énorme de son ventre' (22). On the face of it, then, Maupassant's men would seem to be a rather sorry spectacle.

Having enumerated so many instances of the author's sardonic, satirical approach to characterisation, the tendency is to assume that Maupassant has little positive to say in defence of his male characters. And yet, the assumption would be quite wrong. Maupassant's bourgeois can also show themselves to be proud of their position or achievements: one thinks of Loisel's pride when he triumphantly hands his wife the ill-fated invitation to the ministry ball (2). In a similar vein, we are struck by Jean Marin's comic pomposity in respect of his status as 'conseiller d'Etat', or Caravan's sense of self-importance since receiving the 'légion d'honneur' (28). Many readers might want to argue that Maupassant is still writing in satirical mode here: indeed, the 'orgueil' shown by these characters is a form of hubris, a fatal, almost tragic flaw, which leads inevitably to the downfall of the characters concerned. At another level, however, the kind of pomposity Maupassant is highlighting is a very human weakness, an understandable, if not always excusable, propensity to show off one's worth.

Following this line of reasoning a little further, it becomes clear that many of Maupassant's middle-class men have the milk of human kindness in them. Loisel spontaneously gives up his savings to his wife in order that she may buy a dress to attend the ministry ball. Caravan's grief at his mother's 'death' is presented as genuine, even touching in its evocation of the 'autrefois ...inoubliable' which wells up within him (38). For all his limitations, then, Caravan is not without endearing qualities. A dutiful son, he is also a doting father (31). True, Maupassant never allows us to become too committed to characters such as Caravan, comprehensively pulling the rug out from beneath our feet at the end of the story. But the grieving Caravan, prey to 'l'abîme noir des douleurs irrémédiables' (38), touches us briefly because of the universality of that grief, a situation all of us will have to face at some point in our lives.

In sum, Maupassant has an ambivalent, balanced approach to his male characters. They are sometimes cowardly, yet also capable of sudden courage. Those in middle age may have a tendency to be overweight, but they are not without vigour or the ability to work hard for a living. And so on. In short, they have contradictory characteristics and, despite being in many cases what E. M. Forster (*19*, p.75) would have called 'flat' characters, they are, on occasions, capable of complexity of response. Maupassant's characterisation, then, might be described as a form of rich caricature. While the short story, as a literary form, clearly runs the risk of superficial treatment of character, Maupassant's talent lies in the fact that he is able, within the space of a few pages, to give his characters the depth necessary for them to enter into resonance with the experience of the reader.

Women

So much has been written about Maupassant's attitudes to women (see, for example, *16*, *18*, *25*, *46* and *51*), that it is sometimes difficult to approach the subject without appearing reductive or polemical. His well documented misogyny is universally seen as reprehensible by readers at the beginning of the twenty-first century. Whatever criteria we use to evaluate Maupassant's views on women, there do seem to be a number of powerful and permanent elements in his portrayal of the female of the species which allow us to offer a useful survey of female characters in *Quinze contes*.

Like Maupassant's men, his women are often inhabited by a desire to better themselves which draws them into difficult situations. Mathilde Loisel in *La Parure* offers a good example. Her dreams of grandeur, or at least of a form of social prominence beyond her natural lot, lead to disaster. From a position of considerable material comfort, she and her husband are forced back down the social scale, even to the point of abject poverty. In one sense this is further evidence of the classical approach we discussed at the beginning of this chapter, since Maupassant implies that eternal forces other than those of liberal individualism ultimately govern our relationship with the world. In another sense, Maupassant is indulging in a parody or perversion of a well known tale: indeed, Mathilde could be seen as an anti-Cinderella. Given Maupassant's great familiarity with the work of his literary mentor, Gustave Flaubert, Mathilde Loisel is clearly indebted to Flaubert's great heroine, Emma Bovary. 'Bovarysme', or a desire to be other than we truly are, is what leads to Mathilde's downfall. Her inability, that is, to relate to what is authentic — in herself and in others — constitutes for her a fatal flaw. She goes in search of an illusion, a fake existence and has such faith in fakes that she is returned to a reality which is much more unpleasant than the one she had aspired to leave.

In terms of what we might today call 'gender politics', Mathilde's fate is equally ironical. From a position at the margins of the economic system, one of dependence on and subservience to her husband, she acquires a position of ironical equality with him in the sense that they are both condemned to the same form of drudgery. Mathilde's desire for recognition, her assertiveness, plunges the couple into a form of slavery.

Whether one sees Mathilde's fate as the statement of a classical author, as a sophisticated parody, or as a misogynistic irony — or as all three — it is clear that Maupassant is writing in an essentially conservative mode. Things, the implication seems to be, are as they are and we attempt to change them at our peril. The principle, then, which is being expressed indirectly here is that change is not ultimately possible. People are subjected to forces which are quite beyond their control and there is no guarantee of success when one attempts to go against the grain, against the nature of things.

But to suggest that Maupassant is in some way a satisfied or sanguine male conservative would be wide of the mark. He is, on the contrary, an anxious one, filled with existential *Angst* in the face of, as he sees it, the immutable conditions of our existence. And it is in this respect that Maupassant's treatment of female characters perhaps takes on an additional dimension. For women are, on the human scale, the principal channel through which eternal, natural forces are expressed. Women operate — or perhaps, Maupassant might say, are operated — on quite a different level from men.

Nowhere is this clearer than in the story *Une vendetta*. 'La veuve Saverini', in a state of catatonic grief, vows to take revenge for the treacherous murder of her son, Antoine. She proceeds to do so in the most terrible fashion ('sauvage, vindicatif et féroce' [11]). The calm premeditation of the murder and the cold-blooded nature in which she carries out her revenge is highly disturbing in clinical terms: she behaves in the manner of a psychopath. Within the old lady, a highly developed, calculating, rational capacity exists alongside a powerful irrational drive. What might legitimately be described, at a more mundane level, as maternal affection, is here worked up into a frenetic instinct to kill. The rational human mind, in other words, is placed at the disposal of an atavistic, savage desire. Rather than civilised values dominating the natural forces within her, Maupassant's killer widow inverts the relationship: her exacerbated maternal drive colonises her intellect.

This inverted hierarchy has a broader significance where Maupassant's female characters are concerned, as does Saverini's ability to disguise herself in order to commit the murder. There is something almost bestial about the way in which the grieving mother sets about her task. In terms of a paronymic pun, Maupassant, writing (11) of 'la femme et la bête', implies that 'la femme e[s]t la bête'. In a similar way, Saverini's sleep takes on animalistic contentedness at the end of the story.

Both of these 'female' characteristics — the unstoppable workings of nature and the innate capacity for dissimulation — are typical of much writing by men in the late nineteenth century, to the point where one can almost speak of a 'bachelor style'. It is this cultural resonance which is so difficult for us to recapture, but which is essential for a better understanding of Maupassant's work. Clearly, masculine fears about the evolving role of women in society at the end of the nineteenth century were never far from view. But these were symptomatic of a much wider millennial anxiety about the precise value of notions such as 'identity' and the role and validity of science in general. Gender, or male versus female, to use terms more appropriate to the author's own period, forms a central element in this respect and is a constant issue in Maupassant's writing, present throughout *Quinze contes*. Madame Caravan senior, for example, seems to push collusion with natural forces to the absolute extreme, dying and returning to life, to the amazement and horror of those around her. As in the case of the old widow Saverini, Maupassant's treatment of his subject also necessarily places a question mark over the status of science: Saverini perverts behaviourist, Pavlovian conditioning for criminal ends, while Caravan's mother is pronounced dead by a would-be doctor.

The feminine, clearly, fascinates Maupassant: and not simply in the sense that he was a 'ladies' man'.[6] For Caravan's old mother can also be seen as something of a feminine (if not yet feminist) icon, a female Christ rising from the dead, though here on the first day. Into this irony, Maupassant works another, finer one, that of Braux, 'un cordonnier socialiste' and therefore presumably atheist, exclaiming 'Eh bien, quoi? Elle ressuscite' (47). The male scientist, 'le *docteur* Chenet' (Maupassant's italics, 33) and his 'vagues connaissances médicales' (26) are discredited and Caravan's mother achieves the most profound artifice: that of faking death. Her apparent death is merely a protracted 'syncope', a disconcerting or deceptive pause or break, a change in rhythm. What appears to be the most natural thing in the world — the death of a ninety-year-old lady — is nothing more than a hiccup in her existence. Nature is never more present than during its absence and the old lady's life begins again as abruptly as it had appeared to come to an end.

Female artifice is one of the most important aspects of *En famille*, the story which is the centrepiece of this collection. From the outset the story foregrounds the 'dignité intempestive' of the women travelling on the upper deck of the Neuilly tram (25). It is clear, too, from the start that Caravan is in thrall to his mother and

---

[6] Five of the anthologies from which the *Quinze contes* are taken are named after female characters: *Boule de suif*, *La Maison Tellier*, *Mademoiselle Fifi*, *Miss Harriet*, and *Les Sœurs Rondoli*.

that he follows his wife's advice on every question: the small family unit is, in effect, a form of matriarchy. The transmission of that matriarchal power is assured in the sense that Caravan's daughter, Marie-Louise, 'ressemblait à sa mère déjà, parlait comme elle, répétant ses paroles, l'imitant même en ses gestes' (31). Or again, when his mother's 'death' is pronounced by Chenet, Caravan's wife displays her capacity for artifice through her 'crise convenable de chagrin' which contrasts with her husband's 'douleur vraie' (33). While Caravan is overcome with grief and unable to do or say anything, his wife remains quite dispassionate and sets about organising what Maupassant refers to cynically as 'la figuration qui doit accompagner la Mort' (34). Caravan's lack of attention, however, is quite genuine, as he rolls little pellets of bread and places them on the tablecloth.

Maupassant's insistence on the capacity for organised dissimulation shown by Caravan's wife and her obvious attachment to ritual, represent women's natural tendency — as Maupassant sees it — to operate in an inauthentic, artificial or theatrical mode. Madame Simon in *A cheval*, for example, convinces police, doctors and the courts that she is suffering invisible but permanent injury and acquires from the hapless Gribelin a pension 'pour jusqu'à la fin de [ses] jours' (68) as a result. In the case of Caravan's wife, her punctilious approach to her mother-in-law's death is dictated not by filial duty, but by base self-interest, a fact underlined by the hilarious episode of the removal of Madame Caravan senior's furniture (41–43). We have already seen how Caravan's wife fakes her grief, a 'chagrin de commande' as it is later called (45). She is also responsible for all the details of the ceremony accompanying the wake. The latter, indeed, proves to be an exclusively female affair, since it is Rosalie who dozes next to the 'corpse' all night long. In a similar way, what follows is dominated by women: 'la foule de curieuses' (45) as Maupassant calls them. Even the artificial artifice, as it were, the imitation ceremony performed by the children a little later, is also predominantly female — 'cinq filles et deux garçons (45) — and we are explicitly informed that the children who come to see their defunct neighbour are 'de petites filles surtout, plus éveillées, flairant plus vite tous les mystères de la vie' (45).

The discreet allusion here to the reproductive function is illustrated by old Madame Caravan herself in the sense that her return from the dead constitutes a spontaneous rebirth, as nature, through Madame Caravan, decides that the 'syncope' has lasted long enough. More conventional evidence of female fertility is provided by Madame Braux, Caravan's sister. Her 'ventre d'hydropique' (47) — like a huge balloon filled with water — is an exaggerated emblem of her fertility. What could be a simple statement about Madame Braux's pregnancy becomes a much more disturbing representation of an uncontrollable, almost grotesque natural force. A little later, the point is made even more prominently: 'son ventre énorme encombrait tout le palier, empêchant les autres d'avancer' (48). There is clearly something of masculine fascination and anxiety in the representation of such a hyperbolic belly. It is as though the burgeoning stomach constitutes a threat: and indeed, a little further on, the narrator refers to Madame Braux's 'ventre menaçant' (49).

In short, women dominate men in *Quinze contes*, even if that domination is sometimes represented ironically, indirectly. Maupassant's women are the privileged site of innate qualities of cognition and manipulation which are apparently denied to the author's male characters. It is not simply that the men are deferential to the women, as when Loisel agrees to commit his savings to the purchase of an evening gown for his wife. For it could be argued that Maupassant, here, is merely representing a strong social convention: men, in view of their education, are expected to do this sort of thing. And yet this deference, as far as Maupassant is concerned, is the tip of a much more impressive iceberg: polite conventions, that is, constitute the visible part of an immensely powerful, hidden force. This force is a form of subjugation: of men to women. If one wanted to define this in literary terms, one might perhaps call it the 'Lady Macbeth syndrome', though not all Maupassant's women are such deliberate schemers as the wife of Shakespeare's tragic hero. Beyond the convenient literary reference, however, the representation of women as dominant, manipulative beings has been seen as evidence that Maupassant — and others — considered themselves part of a society which was in the process of mutating into a 'gynocracy', or a system governed by women.

It is women, as it were, who pull the strings. The image is not inappropriate, since it is often women who 'work' men as though they were puppets or marionettes. We have already seen a quite literal illustration of this in *Une vendetta*, where the old widow, Saverini, constructs, or animates a puppet figure as part of her revenge strategy. *Caravan*, too, is clear evidence of male passivity as opposed to female activity. It is woman who harnesses the forces of nature and in the process reduces man to the role of mere 'pantin'. The story entitled *En voyage* provides a further and more elaborate example, since the whole narrative turns on Marie Baranow's control over the men around her. Her servant, Ivan, for example, is 'aveuglément dévoué, prêt à accomplir tous les ordres qu'elle lui donnerait' (83), or 'obéissant toujours sans répondre' (85). The mysterious stranger who enters Marie Baranow's train compartment 'l'aimait, lui, avec le dévouement d'une bête sauvée, reconnaissante et dévouée à la mort' (86). The different social standing of Ivan and the anonymous gentleman mean that the relationship between them and Baranow differs: not for the only time in *Quinze contes*, this is signalled by a literary allusion, the mute suitor being likened to Don Quichotte. Indeed, there is a much broader allusion to medieval courtly love or 'amour courtois'. But the allusion is once again an ironical one, in the sense that the latter-day troubadour contemplates his 'grande dame' (82) from a distance, but also in silence. Indeed, he is expressly forbidden to speak to her. She, too, takes a vow of silence in respect of him, so that their entire relationship is fuelled by an immense unsaid.

Such references to mutism are numerous. Communication is forbidden and Baranow states clearly at one point that, 'Il faut que nous demeurions étrangers l'un à l'autre' (87). The notion of foreign-ness, of course, is central to the story, since Baranow is a Russian exile. Baranow seems to be suggesting that any form of intercourse — sexual or even social — with her admirer, would destroy the illusion which sustains her happiness. This is open to several possible interpretations. First, it is possible to see it as yet another misogynistic swipe by the author: Baranow, like all women, prefers illusion to reality, falsehood to truth, the artificial to the genuine. Second, one might take a more psychoanalytical line and suggest that Maupassant's view of male-female relationships as expressed here is clearly an immature one. The narrative betrays what is sometimes called the 'Don Juan complex': possession of the desired person provides only momentary satisfaction. What is desired, in fact, is desire itself. Consequently, one arrives at the paradox that the constant frustration of desire is essential to maintain it intact. A third interpretation, and one which attempts to place the story in a broader context, is that Maupassant is surely alerting us to a form of exile, a more metaphysical loneliness, which affects the majority of human beings and which the latter impose upon themselves in an attempt to conceal or deny the true nature of their existence. The 'poésie exagérée' which informs the love affair is, in practice, another example of the existential *Angst* mentioned earlier. The veneer of devotion, the ritualistic behaviour of Baranow's anonymous lover and the highly 'civilised' way in which the whole affair is conducted: these are all ways of trying to keep the forces of nature at arm's length. The pathos of such a situation derives, of course, from the impossibility of doing so: Baranow cannot escape death.

The most powerful evocation of the pervasive influence of the feminine in *Quinze contes* and of the dominance of natural instinct over culture and civilisation, is the story entitled *Le Baptême*. We are at once in familiar Maupassant territory. The story begins with images of springtime in the Normandy countryside, of bursting fertility and birth. Everything is rotund plenitude from the 'ventre énorme' and the 'mamelles gonflées' (70) of the farm's sow or the 'seaux pleins de lait' dotted about the farmyard, to the 'ventre en bosse' (71) of the wet nurse. The raucous gaiety which accompanies the Dentu family and their friends to and from the church is, ostensibly, concentrated around the baptism of the latest addition to the clan. But it soon becomes clear that the real focus of the narrative lies elsewhere and that the title of the story is, once again, ironical. For the church service itself is allotted only a few short lines of text: we learn next to nothing of what happens inside during the ceremony. Far from giving us an account of the way in which a new sinner is received into the bosom of the Almighty, *Le Baptême* describes how the young priest who performs the ceremony is himself overtaken by emotion, by an unstoppable surge of parental instinct, 'envie', 'tendresse' and 'sensation' (73).

Le Baptême is a story about appetites, natural appetites, a narrative in which Maupassant mixes humour, irreverence and compassion. It is another tale of Norman country folk, intent on having a memorable feast, their entire conversation being one long, bawdy innuendo. The constant allusions to the sexual act by the guests, male and female, as well as the presence of a baby, no doubt motivate the priest's preoccupation with parenthood. As a Catholic priest his function excludes him, of course, from that role. The reader therefore registers as 'unnatural' the young priest's obvious need for contact with the baby. But it is here that Maupassant's decision to erase all detailed mention of the church service takes on a fuller significance. For the young man is replaced in his original social context, the Norman peasantry, 'un Dentu aussi, lui' (72). Contrary to our first reaction, Maupassant suggests that it is priesthood which is unnatural to the extent that it suppresses normal urges. Those natural needs — whether it be reproduction, eating or, more fundamentally still, relieving oneself — affect all of us. The priest, the men and the women are all placed on the same level, all equal before Nature.

In conclusion, Maupassant's characters in *Quinze contes*, tend to be drawn from the more modest levels of society. Peasants, workers, housewives, minor figures in the professions and their dangerously inactive spouses: these are the categories that make up the majority of the Maupassant population. All seem destined to live out their lives in obscurity and some degree of ignorant content-ment. But they are invariably thrust into unforeseen and unpredict-able situations — as befits the short story form: these are, in a sense, tales of the unexpected. They are tales of the irrational, too, since what the characters live through demonstrates the existence within them and all around them, of the forces of chance, cosmic malice or the omnipotent indifference of the natural world.

4. Ideas

In the previous chapter I attempted to show how Maupassant, writes in a resolutely classical mode, rather than using a more restricted naturalist (Zola) or realist (Balzac) approach. This is not to suggest that the narrative vision of those two authors is narrower than Maupassant's. What I mean by this is that the two older writers consciously apply methods which are tributary to thinking closely linked to the period in which they lived. They both write from the standpoint of one committed to, though not uncritical of, the society they live in. To put the same point another way, writers like Balzac or Zola, seem to have confidence, or at least a pronounced interest in that which is 'modern'. They especially enjoy grappling with the hustle and bustle of a modern urban environment, the opportunities it creates, as well as the injustice it can often cause. They are trying to understand how a modern society works, how people interact: the aim being to demonstrate how everything that happens is governed by factors and laws which are driven by, or emanate from human beings. The key positive value is *change*.

The preceding paragraph, of course, constitutes a huge and hazardous generalisation and I am not seeking to deny that authors such as Balzac and Zola, occasionally in spite of their much vaunted scientific rigour, give us the benefit of their powerful imagination. And yet, by anchoring their literary project in the social, the psychological and the physiological, in the essentially human dimension of what they see, they are, in my view, clearly at odds with the approach of Maupassant. I shall not pursue this comparison further, but merely wish to suggest that Maupassant saw himself as being at variance with the authors mentioned above, claiming a literary lineage reaching out to his mentor Flaubert and back to Boileau (1636–1711), Molière (1622–73), or Rabelais: and further still, to authors from antiquity such as the great comic playwright Aristophanes (450–386BC).

Now, the vastness of this chronological perspective is already a clue to the fact that Maupassant was sceptical regarding the possibility of positive change in individuals or in society. His argument seems to be that only surfaces may differ. And if we confide in or rely upon surfaces we run the risk of being disappointed. As if to underline the point, when it does come, change tends to be reductive. Change drags people down or back: '*Quantum mutatus ab illo!*' (which one might translate as 'How are the mighty fallen!'), exclaims Monsieur Piquedent's former pupil seeing him now in charge of rows of onions rather than rows of pupils or Latin paradigms. The society in which Piquedent lives has, as it were, levelled him down from specialist of classical antiquity to greengrocer, however pretentious the name he gives his little shop — '*Produits coloniaux*' (123). Piquedent's existence as unproductive contemplative, has been brought into line. Any emotional or artistic ideal has been corroded by contact with the limiting reality of Third Republic France: Piquedent is now (as a consequence, again, of the domination of a woman and marriage) another banal cog in the bourgeois, production-orientated, economic machine of the 'mediocracy'.

The changes in the lives of many of the characters in *Quinze contes*, are of a similarly reductive kind. One thinks again of the Loisels in *La Parure*. Their daily lives are altered beyond recognition, from a secure, if unglamorous life, to a hand-to-mouth existence. Change only drags them down. A similar ironical change affects Marin in *Le Protecteur*. Maupassant's brief political satire, indeed, seems to be overlaid with a more metaphysical point, since another attempt to move things on leads only to degradation. Caravan in *En famille* also suffers a humiliating and, for the reader, an amusing modification. Indeed, in Caravan's case, the alteration to his personal situation — once again provoked by a woman — is doubly ironical: the change, in itself a limiting and painful one (his mother's death) is none the less denied. Even the reductive, that is, is reduced. Caravan's mourning, like Mathilde Loisel's hard labour, proves pointless. They, too, have been deceived by some apparently blind but omnipotent force.

This general downward trend in the stories in *Quinze contes*, and elsewhere in Maupassant's work, has encouraged many readers to place the author in that category of artists who espoused 'decadence' or 'fin de siècle' sentiments. Clearly, there is a strong sense of *decay* in *Quinze contes*, to the extent that the existences Maupassant describes are invariably subjected to disintegration, destruction or limitation of some kind. And yet, this is not necessarily enough for us to conveniently tag Maupassant onto the end-of-century decadent movement in literature and the arts. The obvious fascination for 'decadent' artists of corruption, perversion and artifice, is not a fundamental feature of Maupassant's writing. There is not enough of the tortured aesthete in him, or the eccentric, or the social outcast, to be able to qualify him as a fully paid-up representative of the apocalyptic 'fin de siècle'. It is inevitable that Maupassant, whether in terms of his life style or of his literary style, should sometimes evoke various 'fin de siècle' ideas and characteristics: but it would have been unusual, given when he lived and the circles in which he moved, if he had not been close in some ways to decadence and authors of decadent works. But — defining Maupassant in positive terms — there is too much harmony and too much simplicity in his writing to allow us to see him as a decadent writer.

Maupassant makes the point himself, in one of the rare pieces he devotes to the art of writing. His brief, eminently readable essay of 1887, *Le Roman*, addresses the subject of decadence, though indirectly, under the label 'écriture artiste', emphasising the 'vocabulaire bizarre, compliqué, nombreux et chinois' used by writers of that tendency. The French language, he says, is 'une eau pure que les écrivains maniérés n'ont jamais pu et ne pourront jamais troubler' (*3*, p.46). The complicated writing of some contemporary authors, he concludes, is a mere passing fashion and the French language will outlive it easily enough. In arguing his case in these terms, Maupassant stresses once again his conviction that the individual — the individual writer in this instance — is only a minor moment in the much larger context of literary time.

Maupassant's position, however, is not quite as straightforward as the often categorical tone of *Le Roman* would suggest. True, he achieves what he sets out to do, in the sense that the effect of his argument is to distance himself from 'écriture artiste'. He consequently distances himself, also, from a particular form of literary elitism, from the figure of the decadent writer, the 'dandy', the hypersensitive aesthete: those self-avowed superior beings for whom everyday reality was an unbearable insult. In short, Maupassant is keen to distance himself from the excessive linguistic flamboyance of a contemporary (and personal acquaintance) such as Joris-Karl Huysmans (1848–1907) or, in a British context, a figure such as Oscar Wilde (1854–1900). And yet, though distinct from the position of the ostentatiously decadent artist, Maupassant is clearly establishing an elitist position for himself. The vastness of Maupassant's literary time scale and the timeless, 'natural' qualities of the French language as he sees it, both point to a Darwinian frame of reference, to a society where intellectuals are having to come to terms with the most unsettling discoveries of science. To this extent, at least, Maupassant is still a product of 'fin de siècle' anxieties and it is inevitable that he should be affected to some extent by the ideas that were in the air.

Yet there is something in this geological time span which seems to go beyond the idea of evolution — however slow — and tend towards a notion of *permanence*. Maupassant argues that the French language is unchanging: 'La nature de cette langue est d'être claire, logique et nerveuse'. It has not *evolved* towards this position, but has always possessed that 'nature': 'Chaque siècle a jeté dans ce courant limpide ses modes [...] sans que rien surnage de ces tentatives inutiles'. Indeed, Maupassant's argument appears to run directly counter to the decadent orthodoxy: the French language, he argues, 'ne se laisse pas affaiblir, obscurcir ou corrompre' (*3*, pp.46–47). Decay, the degeneration which many of his contemporaries considered was eating away at the heart of the French language and French civilisation, does not appear to be the main source of Maupassant's attitude. Though Maupassant is clearly a conservative and does not believe in the virtues of modernity, neither does he have sufficient faith in the past to want to return to an 'ancien régime'. The past is not a solution to the present. His position, indeed, rather than deriving from any convictions about dynamism — whether progressive or degenerative — is based on the affirmation of *stasis*, or immobility.

The story entitled *Un coup d'Etat*, is a good illustration of this. Following the rout at Sedan at the hands of the Prussian army, Viscount Varnetot — a 'légitimiste rallié à l'Empire' — finds himself opposed in a power struggle, in the small town of Canneville, to 'un adversaire déterminé [...] le docteur Massarel': a republican, freemason, chairman of the farmers' association and, Maupassant adds mischievously, of the 'banquet des pompiers' (97). Massarel has been biding his time, waiting for the ideal moment to launch his take-over bid. One morning Massarel is in his surgery with an old country couple. The husband suffers terribly from varicose veins: 'Ça a commencé par des fourmis qui me couraient censément dans les jambes' (97–98) he points out to an exasperated Massarel, who insults the old man and dashes off with the intention of taking control of the town. What follows is pure farce and we are soon justified in reading the title of the story as heavily ironical. Varnetot refuses to give up possession of the town hall without official government orders to do so. By the time a dispatch does finally arrive from Paris confirming Massarel's new status as mayor, the doctor has already made several burlesque attempts to oust Varnetot. Relieved, but still grumbling, Massarel returns to his surgery where he finds the same old couple he had left there earlier: 'le vieux aussitôt reprit son explication : 'ça a commencé par des fourmis qui me couraient censément le long des jambes' (106). These are the last words of the story. The doctor is returned with a bump to the down-to-earth demands of his 'administrés'. Varnetot and varicose veins put paid to any grandiose political ambitions.

The story can, of course, be read as a highly amusing episode in the knockabout, *Dad's Army* mode. But there is a sense in which the revolution so ardently desired by Massarel, has taken place only in the literal, etymological sense of 'revolution': a complete circular movement. A change which was purported to be fundamental, a change in the French political regime, is subjected to comical deflation. The comedy, a comedy of situation, carries with it a denial: political change alters nothing, Republic and Empire are, for the peasants of Canneville, the same thing. Elitism and democracy appear to be two sides of the same irrelevant question or false problem: who should govern France? In a country with such a strong revolutionary tradition, torn apart by violent internal political confrontations in 1789, 1830, 1851 and 1871, to affirm that political change is pointless is to make a highly controversial statement. Many of Maupassant's contemporaries would have disagreed with him. His position, after all, is equivalent to claiming that history is marginal. The grand narrative of major constitutional struggles is nonchalantly brushed aside by the author.

But to 'deny' change is an ambiguous concept. One can deny or *refute* that change is possible: one can also deny, that is *resist* a change. Maupassant's denial of change can therefore be read as the expression of a desire for change not to take place, a desire born of an anxiety as to what the change might usher in. It remains for us to see exactly what kind of change Maupassant might be aiming to forestall. In this sense, we notice that Maupassant portrays Varnetot as a reasonably dignified, law-abiding citizen, who refuses to give up his position in the absence of official notification, but who does so immediately that notification is received. Maupassant's treatment of Massarel, by contrast, is much more negative. Massarel's initial outburst — 'Vive la République ! vive la République ! vive la République !' — is received with consternation by the 'deux ruraux affolés' (97) in his surgery. Massarel's maid is 'épouvantée' (98). His men refuse to obey him. He is ridiculed by the town's inhabitants and his every effort to express and evoke lofty sentiments meets with spectacular failure. Maupassant underlines both a certain common sense in the people of Canneville, as well as their total impermeability or indifference to ideas, remaining always 'stupides d'étonnement' (106). Clearly, neither 'le peuple' nor Massarel are presented in a positive light and Maupassant's vision of democracy on the march is hardly a flattering one. This confirms what the reader might already have gleaned from *La Parure, En famille* or *Le Protecteur*, where the ministers and civil servants of the Republic are consistently shown in a satirical light. Indeed, this seems to be a constant of *Quinze contes*.

Only a brief excursion is necessary into the opinions Maupassant expressed elsewhere, notably in his journalism, to confirm what we have just seen. Indeed, his articles — or 'chroniques' — for fashionable Parisian newspapers throughout the period covered by *Quinze contes* (1880–86) frequently deal with political issues, more often than not to the detriment of democracy. Indeed, equality is, for Maupassant, a ridiculous concept defined as 'le mal dont nous mourrons' (*4*, 2, p.233) and even a great republican figure such as Léon Gambetta (1838–82) is dismissed as a 'charmeur de foules' (*4*, 2, p.154). Maupassant insists on the pomposity of what he calls 'les Dupont et les Durand qui nous gouvernent' (*4*, 2, p.369) and, on several occasions, underlines that a system of government based on universal suffrage, that is on the notion of number, is necessarily inferior to government by an intellectual aristocracy, 'la partie vraiment intelligente de la nation' (*4*, 2, p.274). The National Assembly — the main chamber in the French legislature — is described as 'cette assemblée de provinciaux illettrés, élus et parvenus par l'aveugle volonté du nombre' (*4*, 2, p.90), while universal suffrage has been dreamed up 'pour l'exaltation des médiocres, l'élimination des supérieurs et l'abaissement général' (*4*, 2, p.370).

In political terms then, Maupassant could scarcely be described as a man of the left, though trying to place him with any great precision on the political scale is not easy. Whatever his ultimate politics, it is enough for our purposes to realise that Maupassant, both as a conservative and as a writer, is struggling to come to terms with the idea that the society he is writing about is undergoing fundamental change. His recognition of the reality of change encourages him to adopt a position of what we might now call 'moral panic', while his clear desire to arrest such change encourages him to assert the existence of a tradition which cannot (must not?) be affected or corrupted by change. Thus, Maupassant's anxiety finds him producing contradictory statements: 'tout change, tout passe' (*4*, 1, p.421) versus 'rien ne change, rien ne passe' (*4*, 2, p.400). In reality, the two statements are two sides of the same Maupassant coin: the constantly changing surface or epiphenomena, cannot alter the basic phenomena, the fundamental conditions of human existence, which are forever unchanging. Maupassant's palliative, that is, to his own anxiety is a question of referring to a tradition of permanence in order to diminish or counteract the paradigm shift which is taking place.

Despite the superficial changes, Maupassant might argue, nothing is ever really new. This is true in the case of literature, he asserts in 1883, affirming that 'les lettres vont de révolution en révolution, d'étape en étape, de réminiscence en réminiscence, car rien maintenant ne peut être neuf. MM Victor Hugo et Emile Zola n'ont rien découvert' (*4*, 2, p.212). Such a comment about two of the greatest French literary figures of the period must have struck contemporary readers as presumptuous in the extreme. The remark would have been the more perplexing for Zola, whom Maupassant knew very well, since Zola had helped Maupassant make a start to his literary career: and also since Zola had spent much time and energy on marketing himself precisely as an aesthetic adversary of Hugo, on the development of the 'experimental method' in literature and on the general application of contemporary science to fictional narratives. The point that Maupassant apparently wishes to make is that intellectual newness is no longer possible. Elsewhere he writes, 'la pensée de l'homme est immobile [...] les limites, proches, infranchissables, une fois atteintes, elle tourne comme un cheval de cirque, comme une mouche dans une bouteille fermée' (*4,* 2, p.402). Or again, in the essay *Le Roman*, Maupassant insists on the sense in which he is a latecomer in terms of literary and cultural history:

> Il faut être, en effet, bien fou, bien audacieux, bien outrecuidant ou bien sot, pour écrire encore aujourd'hui! Après tant de maîtres aux natures si variées, au génie si multiple, que reste-t-il à faire qui n'ait été fait, que

reste-t-il à dire qui n'ait été dit? Qui peut se vanter,
parmi nous, d'avoir écrit une page, une phrase qui ne se
trouve déjà, à peu près pareille, quelque part? Quand
nous lisons, nous, si saturés d'écriture française que
notre corps nous donne l'impression d'être une pâte
faite avec des mots, trouvons-nous jamais une ligne, une
pensée qui ne nous soit familière, dont nous n'ayons eu,
au moins, le confus pressentiment? (*3*, p.43).

Maupassant's essay — this paragraph included — has often been
read as an instance of special pleading. He does seem, in one sense,
to be alerting us to the possibility that the novel which follows the
prefatory essay will not seem an especially original one.
Maupassant, as it were, is softening his readers up a little, trying to
put ideas into their heads which will make it more likely that they
are sympathetic to *Pierre et Jean*. And yet, this is surely not the
most important aspect of *Le Roman*. Paraphrasing these lines, we
could say that Maupassant is pondering the problem of originality,
musing on the Muse, scarcely a surprising thing for a writer to do.
But he is also alluding, not without a certain pathos, to what has
been called 'the anxiety of influence' (see Harold Bloom's study
[*9*]). A writer is so steeped in past texts that s/he cannot ignore
them, in the literal etymological sense of 'be ignorant of': once a
text has been read, that is, it cannot be un-read. The constant
exposure to past texts means that layer upon layer of linguistic
precedents accumulate, so that a thick sediment of lexical forms
bogs the writer down. Wading through all these words, the writer,
as s/he attempts to create an original work, finds that many of them
stick, individual words, but also entire phrases, thus compromising
the 'originality' of what is being written.

This notion of unavoidable repetition — or what is sometimes
called 'intertextuality' — is one which finds its way into *Quinze
contes* at a number of points. Monsieur Piquedent in *La Question du
latin*, for example, is a 'répétiteur'. As we saw a little earlier,
Massarel in *Un coup d'Etat,* is incapable of promoting change in
his commune and finds himself the powerless victim of farcical

repetition. As we saw in *En famille*, Caravan leads an absurdly repetitive existence, always going to the office 'par la même route, rencontrant à la même heure, aux mêmes endroits, les mêmes figures d'hommes' (26). Maupassant is making a sociological point here, since these characters — and others in *Quinze contes* — are examples of the stultifying routines of modern, frequently urban, existence.

But there is also a metaphysical dimension to the writing here, in the sense that these people do not seem to have control of their existence. Routine, chance meetings, flukes and misunderstandings, the unforeseen and the unforeseeable: these are what govern the lives of so many of the characters in *Quinze contes*. The trivial, more often than not, turns out to be deadly serious, while the gravest of events are regularly trivialised. A simple misunderstanding on the part of Mathilde Loisel leads to a lifetime of misery; Jean Marin's failure to ask a few obvious questions of 'l'abbé Ceinture' ends up by covering Marin in ridicule; Madame Caravan's death turns into a colossal joke; Hector de Gribelin's innocent Sunday outing lands him with a permanent resident invalid; for the inhabitants of Canneville the Third Republic is no more important than varicose veins; a schoolboy's practical joke leads to true love and marriage for Angèle and Piquedent; and so on. Maupassant's universe, as it were, is without relief: not only in the sense that there appears to be no escape from the random operations of some blind cosmic force, but also to the extent that the universe in which Maupassant's characters live is without any obvious moral contours. There appears to be no moral high ground, or low ground. The moral landscape is despairingly flat.

Indeed, the impassable limits of human knowledge which, Maupassant argues, fence off our existence from the cosmos which surrounds us, in effect reduce the human dimension to one of permanent struggle: a struggle which is sometimes wild, savage in nature, but which is always unpredictable, or at least predictable only to the extent we know that we do not know what will happen. Maupassant's fictional universe, that is, does not obey laws of reason. Even science, that ancient *scientia* — the human answer to the human desire to know — is ultimately powerless to help. As in *Une vendetta*, science is subsumed by, and placed at the service of, the larger, more powerful irrational forces. Putting the same idea in a different way, one could say that Maupassant is clearly writing in a 'post-Christian' mode. Writing at exactly the same time as Friedrich Nietzsche (1844–1900), Maupassant is just as convinced that God is 'dead'. However, the departure of the Almighty, or 'twilight of the idols', does not correspond to a departure of the human desire for knowledge. Man remains convinced, moreover, that many things exist which he can never know. Science, instead of filling the spiritual vacuum left by religion, merely underlines the extent of human ignorance. Far from producing a cosy, intelligible environment, the positivism or scientific optimism of the early part of the nineteenth century, overbalances into a negative phase and, instead of confidence in the future and in progress, science generates a greater degree of anxiety.

The story *Sur l'eau* is one of Maupassant's most famous and one in which he illustrates very well how human beings can easily be cut off from those landmarks which give shape and meaning to everyday life. As so often, Maupassant begins very much from personal experience — he was an accomplished oarsman himself — and from a supposed chance meeting. The tale related by one of the narrator's neighbours, 'le type le plus curieux que j'eusse jamais vu' (50), really only gets underway after a long preamble, during which the sub-narrator's excessive and passionate nature is emphasised. Alone on the river Seine at night, he decides to anchor for a few moments in mid-stream in order to smoke his pipe. His fertile imagination takes over and the dark emptiness around him soon fills with a threatening presence. In view of his 'nerfs un peu ébranlés' (52), he decides to weigh anchor and set off back up the river. Despite strenuous efforts, however, he is unable to lift the anchor and is forced to spend the night on the river. It proves to be a testing night for his nerves, as he imagines all manner of strange beings about to attack him and finds himself forced to take regular 'Dutch courage' from his bottle of rum. In the morning, with the help of two passing fishermen, the protagonist eventually manages to raise his anchor, only to find the corpse of an old woman attached to it, a heavy stone around her neck.

The story is striking, not only for its classic *in cauda venenum* (sting-in-the-tail) ending, but also for its rich symbolism. The ever present water, with its shiny surface and hidden depths, immediately sets the scene for a narrative about doubles. Even water itself is of two types, the violent but loyal sea, and the alluring, yet dangerous river. Indeed, the ocean is a place of unfathomable beauty where, hidden 'dans son sein', are 'd'immenses pays bleuâtres', or 'd'étranges forêts et [...] des grottes de cristal'. But there are no such mystical, quasi-maternal attractions where the river is concerned. It is qualified as 'silencieuse et perfide' and typified not by direct power, but by mobility, that is by the 'mouvement éternel de l'eau qui coule'. While the ocean is a place of circulation and (re-)creation, the river is a place of outflow, of loss, of finality. The uterine associations of the sea, that is, are replaced by funereal connotations, with the river as 'le plus sinistre des cimetières', the final resting place: not a holy, everlasting peace, but a place where 'l'on pourrit dans la vase' (51). The 'eau noire' (54) of the river further determines the theme of death and decomposition, already pointed up by the silt and sludge on the riverbed.

All this not only paves the reader's way toward the final discovery as the corpse is dragged up from down below, it also constitutes an illustration of the co-existence of the visible, rational world and the hidden 'inexplicable' (54) or 'force invisible' (52) which the narrative sets out to explore. Indeed, if the concealed 'fond' of the river, with its dark secrets is frequently referred to throughout the text — as an extension of the darkness of night which shrouds the whole story — the opposition between surface and depth is clearly also being exploited as a metaphor for the primitive, irrational 'otherness' of the human mind itself. As the narrator becomes increasingly troubled by his surroundings, he is also struck by the fact that 'il y avait en moi autre chose que ma volonté'. This 'autre' is uncontrollable. There is another, an Other, which (who?) colonises the conscious decision-making faculty of the human mind. There ensues a struggle between the rational and the irrational, 'l'opposition des deux êtres qui sont en nous' (54): a struggle sometimes won by the Other, which pulls the civilised subject back into a primitive, pre-linguistic zone. Maupassant, indeed, concentrates the reader's attention on this, referring throughout to the 'silence extraordinaire', or the fact that 'on n'entendait rien, rien', so much so that when the narrator tries to hum and sing, he is forced to admit to himself, 'le son de ma voix m'était pénible' (52). He is reduced, as it were, to a pre-linguistic state. He ends up shouting into the night, but receives only another pre-linguistic response: 'un chien hurlait très loin' (54).

The breaking down of the barrier between the linguistic and the pre-linguistic is soon followed by the erasure of other limits or points of reference. The narrator, unable to combat the other force within him, lies motionless along the bottom of his boat, until he eventually manages to bring himself to look over the side once more. He then discovers that everything except the river has disappeared from view, hidden beneath a brilliant white shroud of mist: 'on ne voyait rien autre chose' (55). From an uncomfortable, threshold position between two antagonistic orders or codes, it is as though the constant pressure of 'otherness' has caused the narrator to cross over entirely into 'une de ces fantasmagories du pays des fées' (55). This 'spectacle [...] merveilleux' is an exclusively animal one, dominated by 'toutes les bêtes de l'eau', the only voice he hears being 'la voix cuivrée des crapauds'. This 'ailleurs', though the excursion is only a brief one, constitutes a moment of relief for the narrator. He is soon returned, however, to the real, lugubrious surroundings of a chilly night on the river. The anchor chain and the sinister secret it soon gives up to the surface, are an apt symbol for the inescapable link between the two warring factions within the narrator's mind: his physical struggle to rid himself of the unknown burden at the bottom of the river symbolises the psychological effort to rid himself of his irrational fears.

La Peur, another tale of mystery and imagination, sets out to demonstrate the same premise. Again, it is water which forms the elemental backdrop to the story. Again, night and the moon reduce light levels to a creepy minimum. Again, the narrative deals with the inexplicable, the contest between the rational and the irrational. And once again, the latter proves to be the stronger of the two... All the barriers in the narrative are passed. There are no impermeable frontiers. Put differently, nothing is safe. At any point, the apparently impenetrable may be penetrated. To begin with, the elements are shown as powerful threats. Out walking late one winter's night, the sub-narrator remarks that 'le froid m'envahissait, malgré mon pas rapide et mon lourd vêtement' (60). It is not simply that it is a windy night. The narrator's body is invaded by an elemental, fundamental force. A little later, as he tries to calm his hosts' nerves, the rational protection which he attempts to put up in the form of an organised narrative, proves useless in the face of 'la peur'. Later still, the narrator himself is overcome: 'l'épouvantable peur entrait en moi' (61–62). Indeed, the whole narrative is a tale of threat, invasion and loss of those means of rational response which ordinarily defend the human mind. Human integrity, in the etymological sense of wholeness, is inevitably impaired: the characters, in short, lose their minds.

Maupassant died in a sanatorium. The temptation to reason after the event — the author did not die until 1893, whereas *La Peur* dates from 1883 — is very strong. Maupassant, the argument might go, was fascinated by madness and wrote some of his best stories on that theme, precisely because he somehow sensed that he himself would one day go mad. An alternative, but equally facile interpretation, would be to say that the author brought madness upon himself by writing about it too often. In both cases, surely, the link between the writing and the condition can only be a tenuous one at most: writers of whodunits do not necessarily become criminals, any more than writers of science fiction regularly report contact with extra-terrestrial beings. The neat autobiographical explanation will not quite do. True, Maupassant's interest in mental disturbance is an acute and genuine one. But in this respect he is perfectly in tune with his time: it would even have been a little unusual if Maupassant had not shown at least some interest in such matters. He was a contemporary of Pierre Janet (1859–1947), whose work on hypnotism and hysteria attracted considerable interest from the general public. Théodule Ribot (1839–1916), one of the earliest experimental psychologists, was from a slightly older generation, but was still active at the time when Maupassant was writing: indeed, *Les Maladies de la volonté*, an apposite title where *La Peur* is concerned, appeared in 1883. There is also evidence to suggest that Maupassant was occasionally in the auditorium at the Salpetrière hospital in Paris, to listen to the lectures given by the highly influential psychologist, Jean-Martin Charcot (1825–93). So was Sigmund Freud.

In bringing this brief survey of the ideas explored in the stories of *Quinze contes* to a conclusion, it is difficult to avoid the impression that Maupassant, far from contenting himself with simple tales, well told, was acutely aware of the changes taking place in the society of which he was a member and was keen to incorporate these into his narratives, to work through them, to try to understand them. From the preceding discussion it should be clear that he was opinionated on many issues. It would have been unrealistic of Maupassant's contemporary readers, and would still be so of his present-day ones, to assume that he (or any artist) can operate in an intellectual vacuum. As we have seen, his stories deal with questions of contemporary history, even of a journalistic character. And yet, as a writer, his main line of approach passes inevitably through expression. His basic views on language, which we have so far only discussed briefly, are clear enough. But in what sense does Maupassant's style function in tandem with the ideas we have just been looking at? Is the *way* he writes, as well as *what* he writes, of central importance? It is to questions such as these that I want to turn in the following chapter.

5. Language

The linguistic simplicity of Maupassant's writing cannot be denied. We are always struck, as we read him, by the straightforward nature of his prose. More rigorous, or sophisticated methods of word-counting soon confirm that both Maupassant's vocabulary and his syntax are in some sense limited. But in what sense? And why?

We surely need to arrive at a clear understanding of what the word 'simplicity' actually means in the context of *Quinze contes*. It is not merely a question of trying to decide in what ways Maupassant's language is simple. We need, in addition, to try to understand the significance of the limitations operating within Maupassant's style. In other words it is not enough to register the fact of his simplicity and dismiss it or remain indifferent to it. Maupassant is either limited, or deliberately producing a 'limited' style to some other end. Many writers, after all, are much more difficult to read, as many of us know to our cost. But they would argue — many of them justifiably so — that their 'difficult' style is a crucial part of their literary enterprise.

We have to admit, straight off, when we start to try to answer the fundamental questions we are asking about Maupassant's style, that we are up against a contradiction: linguistic reduction does not, on the face of it, seem to be very strong evidence in favour of the idea that Maupassant was a rich intellect. Many critics have argued, and still argue, that truly profound thought requires more than the kind of no-nonsense, limpid sentences which Maupassant favours. For such critics, simple exposition and complex mental processes are mutually exclusive. This is a very old dispute, of course. 'Are books better for being simple or complicated in style?' asks K. K. Ruthven (*31*, p.33). The question, once put, is not easy to answer. 'Simple' and 'complex', after all, are relative terms: what appears complex for one reader might not appear so to another one. An argument sometimes ensues concerning the moral aspect of the dichotomy. Simplicity is supposed to bring in its wake such qualities as transparency, accessibility, candidness, truth. Such writing 'might therefore be supposed to have escaped the complex artificialities which blight the hypercivilised' (*31*,p.48). Some people, on the other hand, suspect the apparently casual of being calculated: like Shakespeare's Iago, simple language, such readers would suggest, is in fact saying to the reader 'I am not what I am'. Even if they do not subscribe to the literary equivalent of a conspiracy theory, other readers often point out that, quite apart from anything else, simple language is ultimately repetitive and boring.

Maupassant, for his part — as in so many other areas of his thinking — might well have been tempted to send us back once more to the 'Anciens': the writers of antiquity and the great classical authors of France's past. Boileau's affirmation that 'ce que l'on conçoit bien s'énonce clairement', might well serve as a motto for Maupassant, who, as we saw earlier, expressly sets aside what he calls 'vocabulaire bizarre, compliqué, nombreux'. He expresses a clear preference for the sentence as the linguistic level at which the writer must try to show himself at his most inventive: 'il est, en effet, plus difficile de manier la phrase à son gré [...] que d'inventer des expressions nouvelles ou de rechercher, au fond de vieux livres inconnus, toutes celles dont nous avons perdu l'usage et la signification, et qui sont pour nous comme des verbes morts' (*3*, p.46). Maupassant's definition of simplicity, therefore, seems to turn on the idea that packing one's prose with erudite terminology is no proof of 'style': the latter is a function of the writer's ability to manipulate the syntax of his language to produce infinitely varying effects.

Given that he opts for 'phrases différentes, diversement construites, ingénieusement coupées' (ibid.), however, it comes as something of a surprise to find that, on the contrary, a significantly high number of the sentences in the stories of *Quinze contes*, seem to be constructed in a very similar way. By this I mean that any page of Maupassant's prose taken at random from the collection is likely to yield at least one, and possibly several examples of a sentence whose rhythms resemble those in the following example: 'Une averse de soleil tombait sur tout ce monde, faisait étinceler le verni des calèches, l'acier des harnais, les poignées des portières' (66). The ternary grouping, or three-beat rhythm is difficult to miss. The same rhythm is exploited in the following sentence: 'Elle sauta au cou de son amie, l'embrassa avec emportement, puis s'enfuit avec son trésor' (4) ; or again, 'C'était Mme Forestier, toujours jeune, toujours belle, toujours séduisante' (8). I must stress once more that these are not isolated examples, but typical of a very strong tendency. Ternary groupings are also regularly present at phrase, as well as sentence level: 'vive, ridée, propre' (88); 'un soulagement, un repos, une tranquillité subite' (38); 'une fraîcheur, un calme, une consolation surhumaine' (also 38); 'leur beauté, leur grâce et leur charme' (1). Again, there is a very large number of other examples which could be quoted. The ternary rhythm recurs so frequently that it simply cannot be thought of as an accidental feature of the writing.

But the precise significance of this tic of style is more difficult to pin down than its obvious recurrence. And there are other recurrent features of Maupassant's style which provoke a similar reaction on the part of the attentive reader. As well as the ever-present ternary rhythms, we cannot help but be struck by the dozens of binary structures used by Maupassant. Again, one can open *Quinze contes* at random and find multiple examples: 'sain et réconfortant', 'les boutons perdus et les pantalons déchirés', 'la rigidité de leurs traits, la sévérité de leur allure', 'inconnus et lointains' (all examples from page 75). The technique is easily extended to longer phrases: 'les gros travaux du ménage, les odieuses besognes de la cuisine' (7). There are even examples of double binary groups, that is a longer phrase which is a binary structure composed of two smaller binary units: 'un air de noblesse et de fierté, la moustache brave et l'œil doux' (107).

Once again, the constant use of pairs of terms simply cannot be fortuitous, a fluke. But — again — the inevitable, systematic nature of the technique raises the question as to its significance. Taking both features together — binary and ternary — the need to arrive at some explanation for their role becomes more pressing. One initial point which might be made is that using such limited language and techniques, without being aware that one is doing so, would be strong evidence of having a 'simple' style, a style which is what it is because the author concerned cannot produce anything else. However, in order not to be aware that one was doing this, one would have to be more than simple: one would be close to being a simpleton. Maupassant's constant and conscious exploitation of such features is already an indication that something more complicated is happening. In short, someone who feigns simplicity to this extent is actually doing something which is anything but straightforward and which is actually quite difficult to achieve.

The approach becomes more intriguing still, when we realise that the techniques of limitation which are applied to style are also applied to narrative: when we realise, that is, that it is not just the vocabulary and syntax which is being constrained in this way, but the overall *structure* of a given story. In *Un coup d'Etat*, for example, the entire narrative development in one direction (Massarel's elaborate attempts to enforce the republican ideology in Canneville) is cancelled out by the repetition of the old peasant's tale of his varicose veins. 'Commander' Massarel's pride and his puffed-up ambitions for his commune, are punctured by a simple repetition. A similar deflationary narrative measure is applied in *En famille*, where Caravan's monotonous existence is ironically relieved — by a death — only to be still more ironically reinstated, or restarted, by a resurrection. The narrative that is 'develops', is gradually unwrapped or unfurled, but then rolled back up, each of the changes which have taken place being reversed. Caravan's wife and Chenet are 'undone' by this undoing, or unravelling of the narrative thread. The implication is that the modification was only temporary, that it was a pause in the natural order of things: indeed, Caravan's mother points out that what happened was 'une syncope', or short break in the normal rhythm of life.

In both cases, the effect of the binary structure of the story is to deny the possibility of any real development. In this sense, Maupassant's stylistic limitation introduces a clear technical parallel to the ideas we were discussing in the previous chapter: progress, for Maupassant, is an illusion. But, just as we are required to accept that lexical and syntactic limitation are being engineered by the author, so the structural limitation we have just mentioned is worked into the text as an unannounced way of shooting down the characters' pretensions. The narrative, that is, does not discuss, does not argue that Massarel or Caravan are pretentious, pitiable beings, but demonstrates it by showing how such characters are subjected to, enslaved to the opposite of change: that is, repetition.

Having admitted that Maupassant's constant use of linguistic limitations is deliberate, we now need to make a second point about his 'simplicity': namely, that it is not only deliberate, but that it is a very deliberate form of narrative control. Rather like Homer's Penelope, who constantly unravelled what she had woven during the day in order to protect herself from her suitors' over-zealous interest in her, Maupassant spins his yarn and then un-spins it. There is even a Maupassant short story called *La Ficelle*, in which the entire narrative is about a piece of string (*2*, 1, pp.1080–86). The implication, surely, is that a narrator is someone who, as it were, pulls the strings, winds the reader around his little finger, plays with the reader, manipulates the reader.

For example, one is often struck by the way in which Maupassant's narrators weave into the early lines of a given story terms taken from the same semantic field as the main theme of the tale. The beginning of the story *Une vendetta* provides an example of what I mean. After a brief description of the Corsican town of Bonifacio, the narrative moves on to a distinctly elemental description of the coastline around the town, a description in which the terms 'sauvage', 'écume' and 'lambeaux' are all used. There is nothing particularly unusual about these words: indeed, in line with what we were saying about the lexical straightforwardness of Maupassant's writing, these terms are rather ordinary. But the role of the words becomes much clearer when one realises that they are functioning as an announcement of what will happen later in the story. Widow Saverini's plan to avenge her son is qualified as 'une idée de sauvage' (11), while the dog, Sémillante, foams at the mouth — 'écumait' (12) — as it smells the black pudding which will be its reward for attacking the dummy Saverini has made. When the dog does attack the dummy it tears off great lumps of the face and '[met] en lambeaux le col entier' (12). Later, when the dog is set upon the real target, Nicolas Ravolati, Sémillante tears off his neck 'par lambeaux' (13). In fact, the entire descriptive paragraph on Bonifacio sets up a parallel between the savagery of the place and the savagery of its inhabitants. The latter are seen virtually to grow out of the cliff face, their houses 'ont l'air de nids d'oiseaux sauvages accrochées ainsi sur ce roc' (10). The rocks which poke menacingly through the foamy water, the appearance of which is likened to 'lambeaux de toile', are a very precise premonition of Sémillante's foaming mouth and teeth tearing the victim to shreds.

Any work of art, of course, possesses, indeed is defined by, its fundamental aesthetic unity, but Maupassant seems to be demonstrating the fact in a very pointed way. It is not that he is using what is often referred to as a 'pathetic fallacy' — the projection of human emotions onto features of the landscape — but that he is quite deliberately steering, or funnelling the reader's attentions in a specific direction. The reader's freedom of interpretation, or construction of the meaning of the narrative, is in fact placed on authorial rails. This could be seen as an inevitable consequence of the short story genre: an author has no time for shilly-shallying and must produce his effects quickly. The more generous dimensions of a novel, it could be argued, mean that the economy of expression required by a short story can be luxuriously ignored. But it would not be hard to find short stories, too, in which the reader's search for the semantic unity of the narrative is allowed more freedom from authorial direction. I need to stress that the example from *Une vendetta* is not the only instance where Maupassant is pushing his reader in a particular direction: part of the 'simplicity effect' of his writing clearly derives from this tendency to work into the descriptive passages of a story precisely those terms which he intends to exploit at the level of the plot.[7]

---

[7] In this respect see also pages 29, 50, 52, 58, 60, 66, 82, 83, 85.

The control which Maupassant exercises over his writing extends even to the process of naming his characters. All authors choose the names of their characters. It remains true, none the less, that many writers would claim they choose their characters' names more or less at random, while many others, though they admit the names are significant in some way, have no particular plan in this respect. Even those authors who do make a point of carefully choosing the names of their characters, do not necessarily reveal the motivation for doing so, which can often remain obscure. In the case of Maupassant the names appear somehow prophetic, their motivation being peculiarly precise. The ill-fated Loisels, for example, live in 'rue des Martyrs'. The stubborn, principled passenger in *Un duel*, who refuses to give in to the arrogant Prussian, is called *Dubuis,* or 'Mr Boxwood'. The narrator of *Sur l'eau*, lodges on the banks of the Seine with 'la mère Lafon'*:* given that the story tells of how a woman is dragged up from the depths of the river, the name seems curiously apposite. The name 'Caravan' given to the protagonist of *En famille*, also seems apt for a number of reasons: first, insofar as he is clearly presented as being subjected to a repetitive, plodding, linear sequence, in common with the near homonym in French 'caravane'; second, deriving from this and in line with the metaphysical dimension of the narrative, the character's insignificance in the face of the immensity, '*déserte* et silencieuse' (37, my emphasis), of the realisation of his mother's death.

Such writing, it seems, is concerned above all with security. Maupassant's narrators are indeed like Penelope in *The Odyssey*. For Penelope, we must remember, will have to accede to her suitors' demands when she finishes weaving her own rich tapestry or tangled web. She will, as it were, be 'known'. She consequently exerts full authorial control over what she is producing in order to delay that knowledge. Her un-telling of her 'tale' and her control over her 'narration', protect her from the indiscretion of those who wish to know or possess her. Maupassant's own narrative seems equally secure or discreet. He even builds one of the narratives of *Quinze contes* (*Le Parapluie*) entirely out of an irony of discretion.

Like Oscar Wilde's Miss Prism — who complains that the poorer classes 'do not seem to know what thrift is' (*The Importance of Being Earnest*, Act II), 'thrift' being an obvious euphemism for 'sexual abstinence' — Madame Oreille is described as 'économe', while Monsieur Oreille is forced to accept terrible 'privations' and only gets his 'monnaie de poche qu'avec une extrême difficulté'. In view of such restrictions, it is perhaps not surprising that the couple are 'sans enfants' (88). It is then only a small step to realise that the umbrella of the title is a metonym for the couple's sexual activity, the narrative relating, indirectly, the cruel limitations imposed on the conjugal rights of the hen-pecked Oreille.[8]

Beyond the immediate level of this being another story in which a man, stuck in a boring, dead-end office job, is dominated by a woman, and in which the marriage institution is subjected to yet another biting satire, the ironies of *Le Parapluie* are multiple. Madame Oreille, we are told, has 'un arsenal de principes sévères sur la multiplication' (88), which we can understand as meaning a strict attitude towards reproduction. The fact that the childless couple should be called 'Oreille' is, at one level, simply an amusing name in an amusing story. But as one of the main organs of communication, it is also an amusing choice since what characterises the couple is their lack of communication and, of course, communion: intercourse, both social and sexual. Furthermore, the ear is clearly connected, given its embryonic form, to the whole question of fertilisation, and is traditionally a symbolic hole leading to a symbolic matrix or womb. Whether it be a religious or pagan tradition, the penetration of sound through the auditory canal is not only a preliminary to the sexual act (as in 'whispering sweet nothings') but is also often a symbol for that act itself: the woman concerned, that is, though not literally 'known' by the man (as in 'l'annonce faite à Marie' where the conception takes place without carnal knowledge), is nonetheless fecundated by him. Madame Oreille's frantic attempts to cover up holes in the umbrella thus take on a more precise meaning, since it is obviously her intention to

---

[8] The short story *La Toux* (2, 1, 722–26) is another example of this form of extended irony of discretion.

remain, as it were, *umbrella intacta*. The aptly named *Maternelle* insurance company where Madame Oreille makes her claim, consequently becomes a metonym for the family planning clinic: the company insures against 'l'incendie', in other words to protect those who may have accidentally been, as colloquial French would have it, 'tout feu, tout flammes' or, more correctly 'embrasé de passion'. Madame Oreille herself admits 'j'ai toujours peur du feu' (95).

As one explores ironies of this kind, it becomes increasingly difficult to avoid the conclusion that, rather than simply writing, or writing simply, Maupassant is playing games. That is, rather than trying to produce documents which are true to life, stories which refer in a reliable way to a recognizable reality, Maupassant writes for fun. His writing, that is, tends to privilege the ludic over the referential. He plays around with his characters, as we have just seen in the case of *Le Parapluie*. The characters are subjected to an authorial tyranny which reduces them to mere puppets, as our earlier string-pulling analogies suggested. In *Un duel*, for example, the dramatic title and the neutral, perhaps even serious tone of the opening paragraphs of the narrative, soon give way to a much more stereotyped presentation — the Prussians are 'armés et barbus', the English 'tranquilles et curieux' (20). A few lines further on, from 'Tout à coup, le train s'étant arrêté' onwards, the narrative moves from stereotype to caricature. The German officer who taunts Dubuis, is 'barbu jusqu'aux yeux' (20) and when he speaks to the two English tourists about his military exploits in a neighbouring village, the Englishmen say 'Aoh! Comment s'appelé cette village?' (20). The officer threatens to cut Dubuis's moustache off and fill his pipe with it. The English, described repeatedly as 'curieux', follow the developing battle between Dubuis and the Prussian, to the point where they are suspected by the narrator of wanting to place bets on the outcome. As the train moves into Strasbourg and the Prussian challenges Dubuis to a duel, the narrative moves into a form of absurd farce. The two Englishmen, seconds to Dubuis, chivvy proceedings along and worry that the train may go without them. Dubuis fires a tentative shot from his pistol and kills the Prussian, who lands flat on his face, 'raide sur le nez' (23).

Maupassant clearly enjoys this excursion. The knockabout comedy of the encounter is its most obvious feature. Yet, beyond this, there is a sense in which the story's amusing simplicity is an exaggerated form of what we have been discussing in the previous paragraphs. Even within the framework of caricature or farce, the characters seem wholly devoid of 'characteristics', reduced to one or two epithets and operating on a mechanical principle: as they rush back to the train, 'au pas gymnastique' (23), Dubuis and his two helpers adopt a rigid pose, running along 'les poings fermés, les coudes au corps' (23). It is as though these characters are mere ciphers, empty shells, their limited, jerky movements resembling those of clockwork toys, automatons or — in view of the singular emotion which animates them, a permanent 'joie' — ventriloquist's dummies. Yet none of this means that Maupassant's story is devoid of serious 'content'. On the contrary, there is something more than a little poignant in the allusion to the loss of Alsace-Lorraine and in the collective 'nous' (20) which accompanies it. And the Prussian soldier, referred to further on as 'l'Allemand', cuts a foreboding figure as he holds forth on the grandeurs of his fatherland, his prediction that the whole of Europe would soon fall under German domination, taking on a peculiarly prophetic flavour: 'La Brusse blus forte que tous' (21)... And yet, this is not what Maupassant is placing in the foreground of his narrative: his main objective is, as it were, to wind his characters up and follow their humorous, frantic antics. But is Maupassant not also... winding his reader up?

Another example of this technique is to be found in the story *Un lâche*. Again, the narrative is about a duel: clearly something of a fashionable subject at the time.[9] The story sets out to explore fear: the fear of a man who must fight a duel at dawn. As in other stories in the collection, the emphasis is placed on the irrational nature of

---

[9] In December 1881, in an article called 'Le Duel', Maupassant writes 'il me semble que nous sommes en ce moment jusqu'au cou dans la plus profonde barbarie'. He clearly did not have the highest regard for all those who attempt to repair their tarnished reputations by duelling: 'Le duel est la sauvegarde des suspects. Les douteux, les véreux, les compromis essayent par là de se refaire une virginité d'occasion' (*4*, 1, 350–51).

the fear which grips the young man. Try as he may, he cannot overcome the emotions generated by his predicament and is forced to recognise that he is dominated by 'une force plus puissante que sa volonté' (110). The evening before the duel, he is so overtaken by uncontrollable fear that he resorts to drinking great draughts of rum. This, however, is unsuccessful. He then attempts to calm himself down by rehearsing the movements he will have to make the following day for the duel, but 'il tremblait des pieds à la tête et le canon remuait dans tous les sens' (114). At his wits' end, knowing that he will be unable to give a good account of himself and having discovered by chance that the pistol he is holding is loaded, he turns it on himself and pulls the trigger. Ostensibly, then, the narrative indulges in a fairly refined form of psychological realism and explains how an apparently brave man gradually slides into a frame of mind which drives him to suicide. On these terms, *Un lâche* is not unconvincing. The characterisation is far more 'complex', insofar as Maupassant gives us much more information about what is going on inside the main character: his motivations and reactions are presented in some detail.

And yet, we are aware from the early stages of the story, that Gontran de Signoles is not an entirely rational being. He lives in a state of unreflecting contentment which operates according to very simple principles: so much so that his reaction to the incident which leads to the duel is spontaneous, almost automatic. Indeed, we know from the opening lines of the story that for Signoles, it is not a question of 'if' but 'when' ('Quand je me battrai' [107]). His future adversary, ironically called 'Georges Lamil' (l'ami?), reacts in a similar, unreflecting manner. The customers 'chez Tortoni', push this type of behaviour to its logical extreme when they react to the swearword (presumably, 'Merde!') which Lamil shouts at Signoles. The passage concerned is worth quoting in full:

> Le monsieur ne répondit qu'un mot, un mot ordurier qui sonna d'un bout à l'autre du café, et fit, comme par l'effet d'un ressort, accomplir à chaque consommateur un mouvement brusque. Tous ceux qui tournaient le dos

> se retournèrent; tous les autres levèrent la tête; trois
> garçons pivotèrent sur leurs talons comme des toupies;
> les deux dames du comptoir eurent un sursaut, puis une
> conversion du torse entier, comme si elles eussent été
> deux automates obéissant à la même manivelle (108).

There is an obvious sense in which Maupassant is drawing a quick
thumbnail sketch: his evocation of the physical movement triggered
by the incident is typical of a caricature or comic strip. The
concentration of past historic verb forms in rapid succession creates
an impression of near simultaneity. But beyond this, Maupassant's
choice of terms — 'toupies', 'automates', 'manivelle' — emphasises the mechanical aspects of what happens. The people in the café
react as though they were all components of an elaborate clockwork
toy. In other words, what is most specifically human about the
characters is absent. The movements, that is, could not be qualified
by such terms as 'inelegant' or 'clumsy': for these words reintro-
duce a highly qualitative, human quality which is quite clearly out
of place.

Here, the mechanical dominates the human. This mechanical
principle, indeed, acts as a unifying principle for the story as a
whole. Lamil's insult 'rings' or 'chimes' ('sonna') from one end of
the café to the other and the subsequent movements all appear to be
governed by a 'ressort' or 'mainspring'. As Signoles later contemplates his position, the sound of his clock preparing to chime — 'le
petit grincement du ressort' (110) — provokes in him a shudder
('sursaut'). There are other sharp, mechanical sounds which run
through the story: the 'bruit sec' caused by Signoles slapping
Lamil's face and the 'coup de timbre' or sound of Signoles's
doorbell. And just as the vulgar chime of Lamil's insult throws a
lever which operates the collective reaction of the customers in the
café, so the main character is driven to 'sursauts' or 'tressaillements
saccadés' (111) by these other bells. Even Signoles's brief
conversation with his 'témoins' is conducted in the same trembling
'voix saccadée'.

The temptation to interpret these details as though they were in some sense symbolic of Signoles's fate is a strong one: it is for Signoles, as it were, that the bell tolls. Yet Maupassant appears to be placing the emphasis on the physical, rather than the ethical dimension. The mainspring which appears to fascinate Maupassant here, is the heart: not the abstract, romantic heart of lovers, but the binary beat, the systole and the diastole, the tick-tock of the essential human clock. Whether it is 'follement' or 'furieusement', the main character's heart beats and beats, and overcomes Signoles: he surrenders to his heart, that is to physical, not to moral pressures. It is reflex actions and instinct which kill Signoles. However hard he may try, despite his 'esprit' or his 'volonté', he cannot prevent his body from taking over, he cannot stop his teeth chattering. He kills himself because he is dominated by his animal qualities, because he is reduced to writhing, beast-like on the floor: 'un besoin fou de se rouler par terre, de crier, de mordre' (112). In the end, Signoles ducks out of his duel, not because he is a coward, but because he cannot accept that his irrational nature is more powerful than his reason. The duel, therefore, is evidence of the dual.

Signoles, as we now know, is not the only character in *Quinze contes* to have this exacerbated sense of his own consciousness, of the struggle within him between rational forces and those over which reason cannot exert control. Nor is Signoles the only character who underlines the pathos of this predicament. Maupassant, indeed, returns on a number of occasions to the idea that the human condition is special, is different, to the extent that human beings are aware, are conscious, of the limits which are imposed upon them, of the limits, that is, of their consciousness. Like Caravan in *En famille*, who experiences the 'calme indifférence de la nature sereine' (39), in the face of his mother's death (or what Caravan believes to be his mother's death), Signoles witnesses the dawn of a summer's day whose light is likened to 'la caresse du soleil levant' (111). In both cases, Nature takes little notice of the predicament in which the character finds himself. Signoles comes up against human indifference, too: his seconds pay him a courtesy visit on the eve of his duel and are totally unaware of his mental state. In this respect, Signoles is again like Caravan, who makes an effort to communicate his sense of loss to three acquaintances playing cards in the local café:

> Ils levèrent un peu la tête tous trois en même temps, mais en gardant l'œil fixe sur le jeu qu'ils tenaient en main. — 'Tiens, quoi donc?' — 'Ma mère vient de mourir.' Un d'eux murmura : — 'Ah! diable', avec cet air faussement navré que prennent les indifférents. Un autre, ne trouvant rien à dire, fit entendre en hochant le front, une sorte de sifflement triste. Le troisième se remit au jeu comme s'il eût pensé: — 'Ce n'est que ça.'
> (39)

Not only is there indifference to what has happened to Caravan, but the indifference is incremental: that is, each of the three men is more indifferent than the previous one. The ternary sequence, rather than a progression, is a regression. We might choose, of course, to read very little into this. Caravan's acquaintances are merely living proof that, as it were, after a death, 'life goes on'. But this would be a somewhat impoverished reading. Not only does Maupassant structure the sequence very carefully to bring out the downward trend in the attention paid to Caravan, but there is also a very strong sense in which he is emphasising the near-total absence of communication between the characters in the scene: a theme which he explores in detail in this story as well as elsewhere in *Quinze contes*. This non-communication between characters can be seen as a social comment — Maupassant, in *En famille*, underlines the anonymous nature of Parisian life, with its stultifying routines, its buses and its crowds. But he is also keen to convey a more metaphysical comment: Caravan is alone in the crowd, is alien in the crowd. The feeling of isolation is pronounced: 'il considérait la foule houleuse des promeneurs et le flot roulant des équipages à la façon d'un voyageur dépaysé qui traverserait des contrées lointaines' (27).

At such moments, Maupassant seems to be arguing, every man is an island. Even the most familiar scenes appear strange, foreign and the individual, as it were, is in exile. The significance of the simple language and the repetitions used to describe what happens to a Caravan or a Signoles, therefore, resides in the fact that it constitutes a statement about the limiting duality of the human condition and the non-correspondence this sets up between, on the one hand, human desire and, on the other, the possibilities offered by existence. Ultimately, it is not cowardice which kills Signoles, but his intelligence. He is tied to instinctive reactions of fear and is aware of this, despite his rational decision not to be afraid. The duel, therefore, does actually take place, but within Signoles himself. And he loses. Although he is not afraid, he fears. His suicide is, in many ways, a confirmation of his human status, not a denial of it. Signoles refuses to be subordinated to conditioned reflexes, to animal instinct. The mechanical and the human, for Signoles, cannot, must not co-exist. The springs and levers which command his emotions, the tick-tock of stimulus and response which runs through the story: these are the cause of Signoles' ebbing commitment to consciousness. And yet, the irony of the narrative remains intact, since it is Signoles himself who throws the first lever: his automatic response to the initial stimulus or challenge thrown down by Lamil, is what sets the larger machine in motion, the elaborate movement which leads finally to his death.

6. Conclusion

The stories in *Quinze contes* will always remain, first and foremost, an enjoyable read. Maupassant is a 'good' writer in the sense that the story never fails to give us pleasure and hold our interest until the end. This story-telling ability, as well as the content of the tales he tells, both link Maupassant to a strong popular, oral tradition. Indeed, the clarity and simplicity of Maupassant's narratives owe much to the folklore of his native Normandy: not only insofar as any child growing up in that part of France, at that time, would have known something about this, but also because much of Maupassant's childhood was spent in the company of the people he writes about. Their tics of expression, as well as the standard characters, the simple plots and the constant repetitions which typify folk tales, could not fail to make an impression.

The ability to tell a good story fits one, naturally enough, for some kind of literary career. Maupassant's obvious gift for the vignette, the deft, but broad brush, meant that he quickly became known as a talented provider of bite-sized 'slices of life' — short sections of someone's existence, lifted out of the continuous onward rush of their lives. Not surprisingly, this meant, in turn, that during the brief period of his literary maturity — a period cut short by his premature death in 1893 — and ever since, Maupassant has been linked to a literary movement known as 'Naturalism' which flourished at about the same time.

But his allegiance to that literary movement, as I have suggested on several occasions, never went very far. It is not that I wish to declassify or reclassify Maupassant, whom one always finds slotted into the school textbooks alongside Emile Zola, but rather, and more positively, I have tried to underline the more original aspects of his approach. For while Flaubert was truly Maupassant's literary mentor, Zola was never really more than a 'truc', or gimmick. A letter in 1877 from Maupassant to the young author and personal friend, Paul Alexis (1847–1901), emphasises the extent to which Naturalism was, for Maupassant at least, part of a strategy to break into the Parisian literary scene: 'Il faudra discuter sérieusement sur les *moyens de parvenir*. À cinq on peut bien des choses, et peut-être y a-t-il des *trucs* inusités jusqu'ici' (Maupassant's italics). A little further on in the same letter, Maupassant is still more explicit: 'Je ne crois pas plus au naturalisme et au réalisme qu'au romantisme'. And he returns to the attack in the spring of 1879 in a letter to Flaubert: 'Que dites-vous de Zola? Moi, je le trouve absolument fou'.

The temptation to reduce Maupassant's writing to the combined effect of these naturalist 'trucs' and popular 'tics' is, as I have implied throughout this brief study, a very strong one. Yet it should also be clear now that Maupassant's literary project is much more comprehensive than that. It is the metaphysical, not the physical, which interests him: Maupassant, in the end, is writing about man in the universe, not man in his immediate environment or in society. Indeed, man as a social animal appears to be very low in his esteem. Whether by means of class conflict, individual endeavour or pure chance, Maupassant does not seem to harbour any serious belief in History's ultimate ability to deliver Man from himself. This is just one more demonstration of the extent to which Maupassant and Zola were very different: while Zola — despite the apparent bleakness of his works — is an incurable optimist, Maupassant's intimations of the absurdities of human life never allow him more than fleeting moments of pleasure. He has no obvious belief in any divine presence in the cosmos and was not one of those many intellectuals who, disappointed by science and its broken promises of an intelligible, meaningful world, returned for spiritual comfort to the Catholic church towards the end of the nineteenth century.

In fact, Maupassant's approach to metaphysical problems is a curious mix of classicism and modernism or, to be more accurate in terms of literary history, of pre-modernism. That is, he is a rational, yet sceptical observer of the human condition. Whether his mind is concentrated on questions of human consciousness or communication, he combines the physical insouciance and sexual licence of a 'libertin' with an extreme moral fragility and sensitivity. He is at once drawn to an essentially down-to-earth form of existence, to the tangible, the real, the knowable, yet cannot avoid dwelling upon the unknowable. His 'aristocratic' belief in the importance of the land, of roots, of a sense of belonging, is no longer accompanied by its traditional, metaphysical corollary — Christian faith. Although it is fair to say that faith and scepticism are equivalent, in the sense that they both stand in the same relation to the unknown, it is none the less true that for the sceptic, the consequence of the inability to believe is spiritual destitution. Maupassant, in effect, lived and worked in what was already becoming a post-Christian society.

It was a society which filled Maupassant with apprehension. In common with his contemporary, the sociologist, or social psychologist Gustave Le Bon (1841–1931), for example, Maupassant is very concerned about the role played by the principle of numbers, by 'la foule' in modern society. The uprisings of 1789, 1830 and 1848, as well as the Paris Commune of 1871, had created a rich revolutionary tradition and a powerful myth of direct action by the mob. Maupassant's own vision of the crowd precedes that of Le Bon, whose *Psychologie des foules* did not appear until 1895. But Maupassant is very much alive to the inexplicable, collective characteristics of the crowd and the idea of 'contagion mentale' which Le Bon was to develop later. The crowd is 'une vaste et étrange personnalité' (*4*, 2, p.16) with its own 'âme collective' dominated by 'une sorte de dégagement cérébral commun' (p.17). This mysterious, spontaneous phenomenon effectively levels all members of the crowd down to the same common denominator, a standardised, social self, quite different from the individual personalities of each person in the crowd. In common with Le Bon, again, Maupassant attributes this behaviour to the suggestibility of members of a crowd.[10] In clinical terms, Maupassant demonstrates

---

[10] Like Le Bon, Maupassant was also fascinated by hypnosis and the way in which a human subject could apparently be controlled by the hypnotist, capable of erasing all semblance of the subject's individual will. The two

the regressive nature of the behaviour of the crowd and the extent to which it resembles neurotic behaviour, or what Maupassant refers to as a form of 'folie'.

The power of the irrational regions of the mind, as we have seen, is a central theme in Maupassant's work. Or, to be more accurate, the inescapable duality of the human psyche is what fascinates Maupassant, yet also causes him great anxiety. Whether it takes the form of reduction of characters to an apparently mechanical status, or their enslavement to instinctive or unconscious drives, Maupassant's view of the human mind is a very obvious premonition of what Sigmund Freud was shortly to develop into a theory of psychoanalysis. But while Freud was concerned with the positive use to which knowledge about the unconscious could be put, Maupassant, as an admirer of reason, tends to see the irrational as a potential threat, as an agent of mental *dis*integration, 'une décomposition de l'âme' (58), rather than an integral part of the mind. His lack of scientific training, to be sure, prevents him from properly systematising his insights, but these are none the less lucid for that. His intuitions concerning the non-rational are frequent and, as well as reminding us of Freud, Maupassant, when he is talking of the 'odeur de benzine [...] qui me faisait reconnaître les dimanches' (78), or the 'odeur de fleuve qui remuait dans son cœur des souvenirs très vieux' and the 'buée marécageuse dont la saveur était restée en lui, inoubliable et qu'il retrouvait justement ce soir-là' (37), cannot fail to make us think of Proust, and his rediscovery of the subjective nature of time. But whereas Proust was to construct a vast aesthetic edifice on that founding discovery, Maupassant, again, tends to see it in terms of proof of an 'otherness' or alterity within us, an invasive, involuntary, uncontrollable zone of our being.

Control, no doubt, is the key notion where Maupassant is concerned, to the extent that he sees the conscious, rational mind as unable to protect itself from the incursions of that part of the mind

---

stories called *Le Horla*, the first published in 1886 (*2*, 1, pp.822–30); the second in 1887 (*2*, 1, pp.913–38), are perhaps the best-known examples of Maupassant's treatment of this theme.

which is hidden, which is covert, not open or simple, which, as it were, is not honest or straightforward. All these insidious forms of complexity need to be kept in check, boundaries or frontiers need to be imposed and kept clear. Maupassant seems, above all, to fear the uncontrolled combination or union of the two levels of the human mind. This kind of reasoning finds its way into Maupassant's writing, as we have seen, in the form of references to the liquefaction of self ('décomposition de l'âme'), the melting, or leaking away of the inside into the outside, the 'moi' into the 'non-moi', the individual self into the collective Other. Although there is an important political aspect to this, Maupassant does not fear these things only in the way a political conservative fears collective action. The permeability of frontiers and the subsequent need to render them watertight, means that, as a writer, Maupassant is drawn to a manner of writing whose most obvious characteristic is its neatness, its way of writing about everything, even (especially) the fantastic, in the tidiest, most regulated way possible.

But the need to keep language on a tight rein immediately poses another problem. After all, if one is a writer, even if one believes in control, one necessarily believes in expression, and Maupassant's problem derives from the fact that controlled expressionism is a difficult contradiction to operate and to maintain. How does a writer say exactly what he wants to say while at the same time controlling his style? To a certain extent, we might wish to answer by reminding ourselves that there is a frequent conflict between the constraints of a given literary form — the sonnet, for example — and the urge to free expression: it is even possible to argue that the imposition of constraints enhances expression, since the more demanding the form, the more inventive the artist has to be. Literary meaning is invariably a product of this kind of conflict, or constant search for 'le mot juste'. But, while he obviously faces the same challenge as any writer, such an explanation, where Maupassant is concerned, fails to take account of two important considerations.

First, Maupassant does not appear to be in exactly the same dilemma as other writers, since rather than attempting to express

himself in spite of, or in opposition to form, he seems to be using form in order to protect himself. Language, then, rather than an obstacle to expression, is a screen allowing the writer to limit self-revelation. Second — and following on from this — Maupassant is writing in a post-Romantic context, where the novel and the short story guarantee for the writer of prose considerable formal freedom; and the greater the freedom, the more pressing the invitation to create an individual style, to reveal one's self. Indeed, how does a writer write without expressing, or showing himself? What method or vehicle can a writer use when he wishes to participate in an act of expression or disclosure and yet withhold himself? This is a difficult situation and Maupassant's solution, irony, is appropriately complex.

Irony, that is, is appropriate in the sense that it is intricate, complex, even devious and is used to counter a potential threat from an equally insidious, irrational force. The threat is invisible: one cannot see instinct or the unconscious. Irony, too, is largely invisible: all of us, at some point, have taken literally a sarcastic remark: the traces of irony floating on the surface of Maupassant's prose are equally difficult to spot. This no doubt means, in turn, that irony is an elitist solution to the problem, since only reasoning readers will want or be able to pick it up. Irony, in sum, is the response of the reasonable man to the irrational, a defiant demonstration of the conscious mind's ability to elaborate a protective system which cleverly counterfeits the blind operation of a natural drive.

And yet, Maupassant could never totally deny nature. The well-dressed 'boulevardier' or man about town, was also a country boy at heart, a 'Maupaysan', who, even when he lived in Paris, was an inveterate oarsman on the Seine. Indeed, this seems to be his preferred environment. We can easily imagine him basking on the river bank in the warm summer sun, a straw boater shading his eyes, as he dips his toes into the current and registers the presence of the rustling leaves of an overarching willow. What Maupassant feels for such a scene, I suspect, is somehow what he surmises the scene feels for him: tender indifference. The sensation is at once

delicious and malicious. The abrupt endings to many of Maupassant's narratives are illustrative of this: they are in fact non-closures, arbitrary points at which the authorial guillotine-blade falls and often represent contradictions, inasmuch as the apparent nastiness of the cut-off, is in fact evidence of the grotesque (at worst) or baroque (at best) co-existence of the trivial and the serious, the shallow and the profound, the surface and the depths.

Select Bibliography

WORKS BY MAUPASSANT

1. *Quinze contes,* ed. F. C. Green (Cambridge University Press, 1943)
2. *Contes et nouvelles,* ed. Louis Forestier, 2 vols (Gallimard, Bibliothèque de la Pléiade, 1974–79)
3. *Romans,* ed. Louis Forestier (Gallimard, Bibliothèque de la Pléiade, 1987)
4. *Pierre et Jean,* ed. G. Hainsworth (London, Harrap, 1966)
5. *Chroniques,* ed. Hubert Juin, 3 vols (Paris, Union Générale d'Editions, 1980)

SECONDARY SOURCES

Books:

6. Artinian, Artine, *Maupassant Criticism in France, 1880–1940* (New York, King's Crown Press, 1941)
7. Artinian, A. and R., *Maupassant Criticism: A Centennial Bibliography 1880–1979* (London, McFarland, 1982)
8. Bancquart, Marie-Claire, *Maupassant, conteur fantastique* (Paris, Minard, 1976)
9. Bloom, Harold, *The Anxiety of Influence* (Oxford University Press, 1973)
10. Bryant, David, *The Rhetoric of Pessimism and Strategies of Containment in the Short Stories of Guy de Maupassant* (Lampeter, Edwin Mellen Press, 1993)
11. Bury, Mariane, *La Poétique de Maupassant* (Paris, SEDES, 1994)
12. Castella, Charles, *Les Contes et les nouvelles réalistes de Maupassant: lecture sociogénétique* (Lausanne, L'Age d'Homme, 2000)
13. Chaplin, Peggy, *Maupassant : Boule de Suif* (University of Glasgow French and German Publications, 1988)
14. Cogny, Pierre, *Maupassant: l'Homme sans Dieu* (Bruxelles, La Renaissance du livre, 1968)

15. —, ed., *Le Naturalisme* (Paris, Union Générale d'Editions, 1978)

16. Danger, Pierre, *Pulsion et désir dans les romans et nouvelles de Guy de Maupassant* (Paris, Nizet, 1993)

17. Delaisement, Gérard, *La Modernité de Maupassant* (Paris, Rive Droite, 1995)

18. Donaldson-Evans, Mary, *A Woman's Revenge: The Chronology of Dispossession in Maupassant's Fiction* (Lexington, Ky., French Forum, 1986)

19. Dumesnil, René, *Guy de Maupassant* (Paris, Armand Colin, 1933)

20. Forestier, Louis, ed., *Maupassant et l'écriture: actes du colloque de Fécamp 21–23 mai 1993* (Paris, Nathan, 1993)

21. Forster, E. M., *Aspects of the Novel* (Harmondsworth, Pelican, 1962)

22. Giacchetti, Claudine, *Maupassant : espaces du roman* (Genève, Droz, 1993)

23. Harris, T. A. Le V., *Maupassant in the Hall of Mirrors* (London, Macmillan, 1990)

24. —, *Maupassant et* Fort comme la Mort*: le roman contrefait* (Paris, Nizet, 1991)

25. Hartig, Rachel M., *Struggling Under the Destructive Glance : Androgyny in the Novels of Guy de Maupassant* (New York, Peter Lang, 1991)

26. Hemmings, F. W. J., *Culture and Society in France 1848–1948: Dissidents and Philistines* (London, Batsford, 1971)

27. Lanoux, Armand, *Maupassant le Bel-Ami* (Paris, Fayard, 1967)

28. Lethbridge, Robert, *Maupassant: 'Pierre et Jean',* Critical Guides to French Texts, 39 (London, Grant and Cutler, 1984)

29. Lloyd, Christopher, *Maupassant: 'Bel-Ami'*, Critical Guides to French Texts, 76 (London, Grant and Cutler, 1988)

30. Reboul, Yves, ed., *Maupassant multiple : actes du colloque de Toulouse 13–15 décembre 1993* (Toulouse, Presses Universitaires du Mirail, 1995)

31. Ruthven, K. K., *Critical Assumptions* (Cambridge University Press, 1979)

32. Salem, Jean, *Philosophie de Maupassant* (Paris, Ellipses, 2000)

33. Satiat, Nadine, *Maupassant* (Paris, Flammarion, 1993)

34. Schasch, Nafissa, *Guy de Maupassant et le fantastique ténébreux* (Paris, Nizet, 1983)

35. Schmidt, Albert-Marie, *Maupassant par lui-même* (Paris, Editions du Seuil, 1962)

36. Steegmuller, Francis, *Maupassant: A Lion in the Path* (London, Macmillan, 1972)

37. Stivale, Charles J., *The Art of Rupture : Narrative Desire and Duplicity in the Tales of Guy de Maupassant* (Ann Arbor, Mich., University of Michigan Press, 1994)
38. Sullivan, Edward G., *Maupassant the Novelist* (New Jersey, Princeton University Press, 1954)
39. —, *Maupassant: The Short Stories* (London, Arnold, 1962)
40. Todorov, T., *Introduction à la littérature fantastique* (Paris, Editions du Seuil, 1970)
41. Troyat, Henri, *Maupassant* (Paris, Flammarion, 1989)
42. Vial, André, *Guy de Maupassant et l'art du roman* (Paris, Nizet, 1954)
43. Wallace, A. H., *Guy de Maupassant* (New York, Twayne, 1973)
44. Zeldin, Theodore, *France 1848–1945*, 2 vols (Oxford, Clarendon Press, 1973–77)

Articles, Chapters, Essays

45. Donaldson-Evans, Mary, 'The sea as symbol: a key to the structure of Maupassant's *Pierre et Jean'*, *Nottingham French Studies*, 17 (1978), 36–43
46. —, ' "Nuit de Noël" and "Conte de Noël": Ironic Diptych in Maupassant's work', *French Review*, 54 (1980), 66–77
47. Grivel, Charles, 'L'Entrejeu de la représentation: Maupassant, la science et le désir', *Revue des Sciences Humaines*, 160 (1975), 501–11
48. Harris, T. A. Le V., 'La Révolution et le cercle: la chimère créatrice dans un conte de Maupassant', in G. T. Harris and P.M. Wetherill, eds., *Littérature et Révolutions en France* (Amsterdam, Rodopi, 1991), pp.157–75
49. —, 'Repetition in Maupassant: Irony as Originality?', *Forum for Modern Language Studies*, 25 (1989), 265–75.
50. James, Henry, 'Guy de Maupassant', in *Partial Portraits* (London, Macmillan, 1888), pp.243–87
51. Jennings, Chantal, 'La Dualité de Maupassant: son attitude envers la femme', *Revue des Sciences Humaines*, 140 (1970), 559–78
52. Killick, Rachel, 'Mock heroics? Narrative strategy in a Maupassant war story', *Modern Language Review*, 82 (1987), 313–26
53. West, Thomas G., 'Schopenhauer, Huysmans and French Naturalism', *Journal of European Studies*, 1 (1971), 313–24
54. Williams, Roger, 'Guy de Maupassant', in *The Horror of Life* (London, Weidenfeld and Nicolson, 1980), pp.217–72